# CHALLENGING AMERICAN PROPAGANDA

## TOWARD GREENER GRASS

## EMMETT BROOKS

DEFIANCE PRESS
& PUBLISHING

Challenging American Propaganda: Toward Greener Grass

**DEFIANCE PRESS**
& PUBLISHING

ISBN-13: 978-1-963102-47-5 (Paperback)
ISBN-13: 978-1-963102-46-8 (eBook)

Published by Defiance Press & Publishing, LLC

Bulk orders of this book may be obtained by contacting Defiance Press & Publishing, LLC. www.defiancepress.com.

Public Relations Dept. – Defiance Press & Publishing, LLC
281-581-9300

Defiance Press & Publishing, LLC
281-581-9300

info@defiancepress.com

# Table of Contents

# PART I

## The American Problem

## Introduction

**M**any Americans are dismayed and confused about what has happened to their country. Most people think that bad times run in cycles, and normally they would be right. We've just hit a bump in the road. America has always been one election away from blissful utopia. Some political and economic analysts are predicting a bleak future for the collective West (CW). The CW is driving a runaway locomotive, headed toward a cliff, with no brakes or reverse gear. Many Americans would say they have heard these doomsday predictions and conspiracy theories before.

The intent of this book is not to fearmonger, but to convince those who might listen, to take action and search for a path to greater happiness and fulfillment. Many good people in America could save themselves. No one knows the timing of these events. Many will perish because they won't listen to facts or reason. They are products of a terrible education system, a corporate media that only produces lies and propaganda, and an entertainment industry designed to create useful idiots. Americans don't understand the nature of the government, the economic system, and the culture that are designed to enslave and destroy us. This book attempts to educate and persuade Americans to cast aside harmful propaganda myths, and see a more realistic view of our situation.

This book is not a call to arms. The protected class, the dynastic banking families and their army of oligarchs, have an absolute monopoly on legal violence. They control the police, military, intel agencies, and all the technology. An armed rebellion might have been practical 200 years ago, but it didn't work out well for the Confederate states. Two thousand years ago, Spartacus and his militia ended up being nailed to crosses on the side of a road. The so-called militias, run by undercover police and confidential informants, are entrapment operations. This book doesn't recommend meeting Ray Epps at the Capitol Building, or going to prison with the Proud Boys, or getting deleted.

Some Americans are buying guns and prepper supplies from fearmongering entrepreneurs. While having these materials feels comforting, all this will accomplish is to drain their resources and make them a burglary target. The TV preachers tell us we need to pray and send them more money because Jesus needs a new jet airplane and another mansion. Some well-meaning and naïve Americans advise us to have faith in democracy, get involved in the political process, and attend meetings at city hall and the school board. Most government employees don't care about you, your values, your needs, or the welfare of anyone. What they care about is promoting twisted ideas and laundering taxpayer funds.

The U.S. government is a laundromat with nuclear weapons. The U.S., the European Union (EU) and the British Commonwealth states (Canada, Australia, New Zealand) are organized crime gangs pretending to be governments. These murderous thugs have no regard for human life. A civilization cannot survive such a burden of corruption. The fall of the CW is in progress. It is inevitable, and it cannot be stopped. The Americans who survive may be facing one hundred years of misery and poor living conditions. This is not an accident. This is being orchestrated.

The CW overlords are acting in unison on a variety of fronts. Our rulers are not incompetent, stupid, or miseducated. They have all the money and power. For many decades, they have been turning inward against their populations, and this domestic assault will grow as they become less relevant in a non-aligned world where they can no longer compete or impose their will on other nations. Many books have been written about manufactured black swan events, electromagnetic pulse weapons, economic collapse, famine, bioweapons, etc., all the stuff they control. It appears that the nations under most intense Marxist revolutionary attack are the U.S., the EU and the British Commonwealth states.

Americans' hostilities are accelerating because of identity politics, declining living standards, declining opportunity, no election integrity, and a government that always acts against their interests. Suppose you could go someplace where you would be better treated and have a better future. What if a man could change his physical environment into a more livable place. Not everyone can do it, but about nine million Americans currently reside outside the U.S. Some are abroad because that's where their job is, and they can't wait to get back home. Some would agree with the sentiments expressed here, and don't ever want to go back to that insane asylum. Every government in world history was always bad. Some are better, and some are worse. I left the U.S. for good in 2018, hope to never return, and have no regrets. There are significant challenges living abroad, but there can also be huge rewards.

This book explains my reasons for choosing Thailand. This country is a fascinating place, and Thai people aren't hostile and mean.

Most of the Westerners in Thailand are retirees living on pensions and other retirement assets. They come here because the weather is warm, the food is good, and the cost of living is affordable. There are many beautiful women here who are not infected with toxic feminism, and they don't hate white men. Many young Westerners are also living here, doing a wide range of activities, some earning a good living because they have skills, ambition, and an entrepreneurial mindset. A lot of western expats will, at some point, work as English teachers. Teaching English gives us a starting point, a place to go, and something useful to do while we assimilate. The salary is typically small, but enough to preserve one's savings. There is a continuing global demand for English teachers because English is the international business language. It is the language of the British Empire. A lot of young Westerners who have lived abroad had a good time, acquired teaching experience, learned a foreign language, and ended up with enviable corporate careers. Not everyone can be a teacher. It requires skills, which are learnable, that employers value. The final section of this book presents suggestions for becoming a successful foreign English teacher.

Many books have been written about Westerners teaching English in Thailand, but this book is non-fiction. There are no tall tales of adventure, heroic violence, or derring-do. There are no exciting stories about sexual encounters with exotic women or ladyboys. Some definitions and history lessons are presented, which Americans find boring, but these are necessary to tell this story about how we got to where we are.

Some people will find this book to be politically incorrect and offensive. The author doesn't wish to cause anxiety or emotional distress for delicate people. This book is filled with conspiracy theories. A conspiracy theory is any information that disagrees with the Central Intelligence Agency (CIA's) approved propaganda and narratives. The CIA invented this term in the 1960s to describe speech which does not agree with the lone gunman and magic bullet narrative they promote. A conspiracy theory isn't necessarily false. It just doesn't agree with authoritarian propaganda, which is always a lie.

## Banned Words

Many words are being banned by the woke word police, and over-use of certain words can result in one's written work being flagged by censorship algorithms as violent hate speech. I hope the following word substitutes are acceptable.

Freem*son = Freeloader
gen*cide = ethnic cleansing
Isr*el = Canaan
J*w = Chosenite
k*ll or m*rder = delete
N*ZI = NATS
ped*phile = MAP (minor attracted person)

## Propaganda

Propaganda is information, especially of a biased or misleading nature, used to promote or publicize a particular cause or point of view. "Biased or misleading" means it is information that is not true—it is a lie. "Used to promote or publicize" means it is a lie told by an institution or a group of people, such as government, a company, a religious organization, an educational institution, a research institution, a news media outlet, Hollywood, etc. "A particular cause or point of view" means there is a desired result this group wants to achieve for themselves.

Propaganda is normally conveyed through an individual—the White House Press Secretary, a salesperson, doctor, scientist, preacher, reporter—and this individual represents, or is the spokesperson for, a larger group of people. The spokesperson can be chosen for different reasons. This person is trusted by the audience because of his past performance or reputation as someone who is highly knowledgeable about the "cause or point of view." Having credentials like university degrees or awards helps to reinforce audience trust of the spokesperson. Having a pleasant and expected appearance also reinforces trust. Having good oratory skills, as opposed to someone who mumbles and looks at the floor, is an important reinforcer. In many cases the spokesperson is chosen because he is a convincing liar. Propaganda is a special category of lying. A group of like-minded people want to achieve a result or benefit for themselves through deception. A student of occultism might say that propaganda is a type of group magic used to control people. The rulers of our world are masters of propaganda and human psychology. Their ancestors have been doing this since before written history.

California Governor Gavin Newsom is a master spokesperson. He always looks polished and put together. He's consistent with his appearance. He always looks the same, so people are not distracted from his messaging. He always looks like what people expect. He stands straight and tall, with his shoulders back and his head held high, and he looks people in the eye, and never flinches. He is a paragon of self-confidence, which he projects forcefully. When he speaks, he uses short sentences, simple vocabulary, a measured tone and cadence, and no filler words. He doesn't distract the audience by talking with his hands or flailing about. He keeps his hands at his side and uses small gestures. He's always smiling, which projects friendliness and positivity. People are mesmerized by this man, and they love to hear him lie. He lies predictably and constantly, and people love the message. He wasn't born this way. He is the product of intense coaching and training. Deception is an art and science that requires diligent study and practice. Governor Newsom is a master of the art of deception. One could say he's a wizard. Women can also be convincing liars, but no one alive is better than Mr. Newsom. He could be a successful Hollywood actor if he wanted. Some voters think he looks and sounds like a grifter and a con man. He is Nancy Pelosi's nephew. G*d help us if this man becomes president.

Many, if not all, cable TV news opinionators are from privileged backgrounds. Anderson Cooper's mom was Gloria Vanderbilt, an heiress and fashion designer. Mika Brzezinski's father was Zbigniew Brzezinski, Jimmy Carter's national security adviser. Rachael Maddow's father was a successful California attorney. They are red diaper babies. Their parents and grandparents were founding members of the Democratic Socialists of America and other leftist organizations. They were raised on Marxism, political revolution, and occultism. They were born into the club. Every major news outlet has a CIA editor who approves narratives and decides what information gets censored. Christian Amanpour is an obvious intelligence asset. Anderson Cooper and Tucker Carlson have both said their college applications to the CIA were denied.

Tucker Carlson has carved out a large media market share by telling the truth about certain subjects the rest of the media always lie about. He has gained the trust of conservative Americans. The media industry is so dishonest that a truth teller is new and refreshing. In a world full of lies, many people crave the truth. He seems to strongly believe certain propaganda myths, and this might not be an act. He believes that America's founding fathers were righteous Christians who promoted human rights and all this other mythical nonsense. The American founders were slave owners and occultists, and this is well documented. Abraham Lincoln and his wife held seances inside the White House. Tucker believes in Manifest Destiny. But it seems like he is beginning to question the Indispensable State. Tucker's job is to reinforce the We-the-People myths. This is our country. You can't treat us this way. We pay your salaries. That house of Congress is the people's house. That's my house, mine.

Tucker thinks elections are still relevant. He often does the patriotic hero worship ritual. Thank you for your service. (Thank you for risking your life to delete sandal-wearing brown people on the other side of the world, and taking their stuff, so that we can feel safe, and U.S. oligarchs can further enrich themselves.) Thank you for protecting our vision of democracy and freedom. Reinforcing propaganda myths is his business model. White Americans will never let go of their propaganda myths, and he knows this. Tucker is actively selling the idea that space aliens are a supernatural phenomenon. He has become the trusted spokesperson for the space alien religion. He also seems intent on convincing Trump to choose a certain female socialist democrat to be his vice president. Tucker looks like controlled opposition and a conservative gatekeeper. He controls the boundaries of what conservatives are allowed to believe.

Propagandists use a large number of techniques to spin lies and influence public opinion. *Agenda setting* promotes the importance of a topic by talking about it frequently and prominently. Russia this. Russia that. Russia, Russia, Russia, all day and all night. *Appeal to fear* seeks to build support by instilling anxiety and panic in the general population. We have to fight them over there, so we don't have to fight them here. After Russia defeats Ukraine, they will soon march on Paris.

*Appeal to prejudice* attaches value or moral goodness to something. Israel is the only democratic country in the Middle East. *Inevitable victory* invites those not already on the bandwagon to join in for a certain victory. Staying on the bandwagon is the best choice for those already on board. Ukraine is winning the war. *Join the crowd* says that a program is part of a mass movement, and it is in your best interest to join. Everyone is buying bitcoin, and if you invest quickly, you can get rich like them. The *beautiful people* technique uses famous or attractive people to sell a product. You too will be happy and successful if you buy this product.

People are more likely to fall for a *big lie* than a small one. Carbon dioxide is a poisonous gas. The *plain folk* technique attempts to convince the audience that an opinion reflects the common sense of the masses. The spokesperson might wear a flannel shirt and speak with a rural accent. The *cult of personality* uses mass media to create an idealized and heroic public image with flattery and praise. Political campaigns pay the media to produce flattering interviews and opinion articles, puff pieces, about all the wonderful accomplishments and future plans of their candidate. *Demonizing the enemy* makes the opposition appear to be sub-human, worthless or immoral. Putin is an evil dictator who eats children for breakfast. *Demoralization* is propaganda directed at the enemy to encourage surrender or defection. Polling data shows that Hillary is way ahead, so Trump supporters shouldn't waste their time voting for that loser. *Disinformation* is the creation or deletion of information using fake photos, videos, audio recordings and public records. The Steele dossier proves that Trump is a Putin puppet. *Divide and rule* gains and maintains power by breaking up larger concentrations of power that individually have less power than the one implementing the strategy. Countries that do not vote with us in the General Assembly, are part of the axis of evil.

*Euphemism* replaces offensive, or harsh sounding words with more pleasant-sounding words. Murdered civilians are reported as collateral damage. Genocide is ethnic cleansing.

*Euphoria* uses a happy or appealing event to boost morale. People like military parades with marching bands and patriotic messages. *Firehose of falsehood* is when a large number of messages are broadcast rapidly, repetitively and continuously over multiple channels of news and social media. Conservatives are racists; they want to kill us, and they are enemies of democracy and freedom. *Flag waving* justifies an action on the grounds that it makes one more patriotic, or it will benefit the country in some way. We have to send more money and weapons to Ukraine to defend democracy and freedom. Uncle Sam needs your children to fight for democracy and freedom. *Glittering generality* uses emotionally appealing words to associate an idea or product with an already established feel-good value. Hope and change are going to transform our nation into a socialist utopia. *Guilt by association* is used to get the target audience to disapprove of an action or idea by suggesting it is popular among disliked groups. The Second Amendment should be abolished, because conservatives like guns.

A *half-truth* is a deceptive statement that contains some element of the truth. The Pal*stinians don't have food to eat. *Intentional vagueness* is saying something so vague that it's meaningless or open to several interpretations, with the intent of distracting from legitimate concerns or questions. Inflation is transitory. We will control inflation with more deficit spending. *Labeling* describes someone or something with a derogatory word or phrase. The Russians are drunks, and Zelensky is a cocaine addict. *Limited hangout* happens when someone's secret is revealed, and he admits to some of the truth while holding back other damaging information. I did not inhale, and I did not have sex with that woman. *Love bombing* is used to recruit someone by bombing him with attention and affection. I knew you were the perfect person for our organization the moment I met you.

*Repetition* of certain symbols or slogans helps audiences remember them. Make America great again. *Scapegoating* is assigning blame to someone for the wrongdoings of others. It's Bush's fault. A *smear campaign* is an effort to undermine someone's reputation. A porn actress said she had an affair with Trump. *Testimonials* are quotations from people cited to support an idea or product. Let's listen to Bob talk about how much better he feels after taking this drug. *Gaslighting* means to manipulate someone into doubting their own perceptions, experiences or understanding of events. If you don't vote for me, then you're not black. Anyone who doesn't think this is the greatest economy in history—is crazy.

Censorship is the suppression or prohibition of information that is considered politically unacceptable or a threat to national security. Government and media use censorship every day to mislead the public into believing things that are not true. They leave out critical information that would contradict the narrative they are promoting. When the media shows scenes of dire poverty in Africa, they conveniently forget to inform us that these are French colonies under French military occupation. They don't tell us these poor people have been enslaved, and had their resources stolen by France for decades. This information is critical to understanding the truth, so it is not reported—it is censored. The media never told us that: Yasser Arafat was a billionaire Freeloader; Vietnam was a French slave colony for one hundred years; Osama bin Laden was a CIA asset named Tim Osman; or that ISIS is a CIA contractor. They never told us JFK was shot from the front, although Walter Cronkite said exactly that minutes after the Parkland doctors gave their press conference. President Trump told us that he would unseal: the twenty-seven pages redacted from the 911

Commission Report; the JFK assassination records; and the FISA court records—this information remains censored. FISA stands for Foreign Intelligence Surveillance Act of 1978.

Modern propaganda was pioneered by Edward Bernays, who was a nephew of the famous psychoanalyst Sigmund Freud. Bernays described the masses as irrational and subject to herd mentality, and he outlined ways that skilled practitioners could use crowd psychology to control people in desired ways. He consulted with major corporations, government agencies, and politicians. Joseph Goebbels effectively applied these methods.

Humans are very susceptible to propaganda. When I was about five years old, I strongly believed in the Santa Claus myth. A trusted spokesperson, my mother, told me about this myth, and I believed her. I was surrounded by reinforcers of the myth. There were animated Christmas cartoons on TV. On Christmas Eve night, the weather man would report public sightings of the reindeer and the sleigh flying through the clouds, so I knew I better get to bed because Santa only comes when you are sleeping. I thought about some of the naughty things I had done, and hoped Santa wouldn't hold back on any of the gifts I wanted. I had a coloring book with Santa and the reindeer. We had a Christmas tree. My mom would put out a snack, like a cookie, for Santa because he had a big job, and he had to work all night. Santa's presents would show up under the tree every year. All my classmates and teachers were believers. We did Christmas activities, made decorations, and sang Christmas songs. Some older kids in my neighborhood told me Santa was all a big lie. I was angry. I even cried, because they mocked me like I was some stupid little kid. I told those boys they were liars. I had proof that Santa was real. This was such a trauma that I remember it all these years later. Those mean boys popped my propaganda bubble. I didn't realize what a spoiled little kid I was until I met my wife. She never got a present or a cookie. Today she's wealthy. When she wants a present, she does something on the Internet, and Santa brings it to her driveway—Thai homes don't have chimneys. Maybe this will help her deal with her childhood traumas.

*Magic* is the use of deception to get what one wants from people. When someone pays money to see a magic show, they are deceived with illusions, and the magician gets what he wants, the money. The same can be said about a Hollywood movie—you pay them money, and they deceive you with their manipulation agenda. When you listen to a salesman, a fortune teller, or a politician, you may be exposing yourself to magic. Druidic and Celtic wizards carried a staff made from the Holly tree, Hollywood. Disney is the magic kingdom where lies are transformed into belief.

*Black magic* is the use of deception to get people to do what is against their own interests. When you watch a TV drug ad, or listen to a TV preacher, or a military recruiter, or a psychopathic narcissist, you are definitely exposing yourself to black magic. They lie to you, and manipulate you to do something that could cost you your life or your money, and they get what they want. Black magic sometimes involves the use of drugs or poisons (alchemy). There's nothing supernatural going on here. This is human psychology and manipulation, and that's all it is. It's an ancient art and science. This is the secret wisdom carried down through the ages. This is what hood-winked fools pay a lot of money for, and it's all a scam to teach them how to be Freeloaders.

In some cases, you might be exposing yourself to an *occultist*. An occultist is a person who believes in or practices occultic arts, such as magic, astrology, alchemy (drugs and poisons), necromancy (talking to dead people), fortune telling, palm reading or other activities, while claiming the use of secret knowledge or supernatural powers or agencies. These people belong to occult secret societies, and attend meetings with like-minded people. It's kind of like a church. They swear blood oaths of secrecy and loyalty to their lodge or coven. Together, they practice occult rituals, which are the tie that binds. This is a complicated subject that most people don't understand, don't believe, don't know about, and don't want to hear about. This is the secret religion of the oligarchs, almost all the middle managers, and increasingly, American society. People who want to join the club for money and fame, must join the cult.

# Protected Class

Who are the people running things? Who is that wizard behind the curtain? Many books have been written about them. There is no evidence to suggest they are reptilian, interdimensional shape-shifters, or supernatural entities with horns and red tails, or space aliens. The evidence proves they are human beings. Their wives give birth to human babies. They suffer from human illnesses; they bleed human blood; and they are treated with similar medical technologies.

In fact, we are the experimental lab animals that make it possible for them to benefit from advanced drugs and medical technologies. They only use drugs that have been human tested. We the people take experimental drugs. The U.S. and New Zealand are the only two nations that allow drug companies to promote their products directly to the consumer. When an American tells his medical doctor (MD) that he wants a prescription for a drug he saw advertised on television (TV), the MD is happy to oblige because he gets a kickback, and the pharmaceutical company gets a volunteer experimental research subject at no cost. The MDs harvest the deceased patient's medical data, and collect another fee from Big Pharma on the back end. Big Pharma pays a little money to get the research data, and the test animal is free because he volunteered to be a research subject when he asked for that drug. Concentration camps are expensive, but TV ads are cheap. This seems like a new and improved method, but most countries don't allow this practice because non-medical people are not trained to diagnose diseases and medical conditions. Most osteopathic doctors (DO) probably do not go along with this profit scheme. I digress.

There are theories about the Merovingians, Phoenicians, Canaanites, the Tribe of Dan, the Khazars, the Ashkenazi, and, of course, the J*ws. The historical record for some of these theories is thin and murky. The DNA evidence is likewise not conclusive. However, the history of the Bavarian Illuminati is more recent; much is known about them; and it's fascinating. It's generally not constructive to talk about racial, religious or ethnic identities; in fact, this type of rhetoric can be dangerous. What we should talk about is a person's behavior, and its effect on society, regardless of ethnicity or religion, but we'll never live in a world like that. The evidence shows that the ruling class is a melting pot of Europeans, Americans, Catholics, Jews, Protestants, probably a few Asians, some Arabs, and there is definitely some African DNA in the mix, even if no one will admit to it. Their public religious affiliation is usually determined by location. King Charles is Anglican. The Venetian Black Nobility are Roman Catholic. The Jesuit General is Roman Catholic. Fidel Castro was Roman Catholic. The Rothschilds, who founded modern Isr*el, are J*wish. But people are often not what they say they are. The ruling class is not some monolithic, heterogenous group. In the past, their ancestors were divided along racial and religious lines, and they tried to maintain their aristocratic bloodlines by marrying their cousins, nieces and sisters, which preserved family wealth, and created genetic abnormalities. A lot of books have been written and movies produced about the endless wars between European nobles. In order to accomplish their global domination goals, they found it necessary to form a united nations of organized crime families. That's what the Italian mafioso gangs did in the 1970s. The mafioso families had meetings where they decided they could all gain more power and wealth by collaborating instead of deleting each other.

The ruling class continues to use race and religion to divide and conquer the rest of humanity. Race and religion are valuable human constructs. Their ancestors invented most modern religions to divide, conquer and control us. Personally, they aren't bothered much about religion. They resemble the Romans, who built temples for every known religion. They even had a temple for no god—perhaps these were agnostics. Modern science shows that *homo sapiens* are hybrid creatures. There has been a lot of interbreeding through the ages. We differ by a few genes here and there, but most of our DNA is the same.

What these people do is more important than who they are. Their names are rarely mentioned in the media, and they are very private and secretive. They hate the human race. They are equal opportunity haters. They hate us all. Prince Philip of Edinburgh once said he wanted to be reincarnated as a lethal virus. He was just joking around at a party, but what kind of people make jokes like this? They have a neo-Malthusian ideology. Eugenics and gen*cide are always on the menu. They think of us as sheep and cattle, because most of us act like animals, and, sometimes, we are their food. They have a shared religion. They are all practitioners of occultism and black magic. The occult rituals are the tie that binds. This is a dangerous collection of aristocrats.

Our rulers like big, secret science projects. A new development in physics has the potential to yield unlimited power. They established the European Council for Nuclear Research (CERN), also known as the Large Hadron Collider. They have the High Frequency Active Auroral Research Program (HAARP) to create weather phenomena. They have technology to stimulate earthquakes where there are fault zones. President Trump knows about these things, and the media mocked him for it. The ruling class fund large science projects in Antarctica, where they need less security. They have many bioweapons labs—maybe Prince Philip's wish will come true.

In a 1926 interview with *Collier's,* Nicola Tesla talked about his new wireless technology, and he said airplanes were outdated technology. He wasn't talking about jet propulsion. His life's work was about electromagnetism. In another interview that same year, he described "anti-gravity propulsion," without using those words, and said it was going to revolutionize air travel. He said that this new air travel technology would not use jet or rocket fuel. He developed it, and now they have it. I would not be surprised to learn that the British Dukes ride around in UFOs for entertainment. The American robber barons treated Tesla with contempt because he wasn't a member of their cult, and his free-energy technologies represented a threat to their business model. For this reason, the Germans were the first to get anti-gravity technology. Today's UFOs fly in and out of facilities controlled by Lockheed Martin and Raytheon. The majority of UFO sightings have occurred over the U.S. and Britain. Bush the Elder told Bill Clinton that his security clearance was too low for him to be read into this special access program. This program is managed at the highest levels of global government.

More than once, Elon Musk has said he has seen no evidence of extraterrestrial life on Earth. It's rumored there are gene splicing labs that create human-animal hybrids (space aliens). These creatures might have useful mental or physical abilities, or they might be better slaves if they lack free will—the possibilities are endless. Since they are not human, they don't have human rights. I have personally seen a lot of space aliens on TV and in Hollywood movies. I think a new religion is in the making.

Millions of Americans now say they "believe" in space aliens.

It's been said that the only way to keep a secret is if two people know it, and one of them dies. These research facilities are surrounded by layers of military and private security forces. No one gets in, and the cost of a photo could be life ending. Everyone prefers carrots to sticks. The scientists who work on these compartmentalized projects are well compensated, but they live with an unimaginable fear. The researchers, and anyone who works around these facilities, have signed non-disclosure agreements, and have been told that if they ever talk to anyone, the last thing they will see is their family members being tortured to death. They don't discuss their work with their wives, and they don't go to bars. The protected class are masters at controlling the human mind. They have methods to create an undetectable, mind-controlled slave (Scientology). They have the power of life and death.

# Oligarchs

The oligarchs are the executive managers who report to the ruling class. They manage corporations that are useful to the goals of the ruling elites. They create new technologies to further enable human enslavement, control and depopulation. They own and control the banking industry. They own and control the media corporations that tell people what to think and believe. They manufacture pharmaceuticals and vaccines. They own and control the energy industry. They own and control the politicians who can't get elected without their money. They are very public people whose names are always in the media. They are the public face of the rulers who prefer to stay in the shadows. The oligarchs practice occultism and black magic. The occult rituals are the tie that binds.

The oligarchs manufacture the weapons needed for perpetual war, and they collaborate with the intelligence agencies who run the CW governments. They are the military industrial complex (MIC). They are also a major reason why the U.S. military can't win a war, especially not against a peer military. The U.S. MIC is focused on maximizing profits by producing high-cost systems, in relatively small quantities, while eliminating capacity for large scale production. The U.S. MIC was designed for conflicts against third-world militaries with no air defense. The U.S. MIC is profit driven. Profits are prioritized over national security. The middle managers believe they can fight two peer militaries at the same time, possibly the result of too much cocaine. Think tanks, like the Rand Corporation, are always optimistic that the U.S. will easily defeat any nation that has mineral resources they want to steal. The U.S. military budget is more than the next nine largest nations combined. Some profits are diverted to political campaigns to incentivize U.S. politicians to orchestrate more wars—a "self-licking ice cream cone." The U.S. invades smaller nations to steal natural resources and enrich the oligarchs. The U.S. MIC is a massive laundromat. For decades the U.S. government (middle managers) wasted public resources for war profiteering and nation building to enrich the laundromats located around Washington D.C. Politics are the second major reason why the U.S. military will never win a war. Militarism is a huge waste of resources that excludes investing for the public good.

A laundromat is an establishment with coin-operated machines that wash and dry clothes. It also refers to a business used to disguise illegally obtained financial assets. Cash money from criminal activity is transformed into legal business profits which can then be invested in real estate or some other legal investment. Small-time gangsters used to buy laundromats in large numbers because they are cash businesses. The illegal cash is "washed" in with the legal revenue and then deposited at the bank. With creative accounting methods, almost any business can be used for laundering illicitly obtained money. Religions are the best laundromats because the profits are tax free and the accounting is simple. The intel agencies derive much of their funding from trafficking drugs and human slaves. Shell banks and shell companies are created to move this money around and get it into the black budgets without detection.

Winning or losing is a matter of perspective. When the Soviet military withdrew from Afghanistan in 1988, they took all their military equipment back to Russia. When Joe Biden abandoned $85 billion in military hardware in Afghanistan, this was a victory for the U.S. MIC. All that stuff has to be replaced. They socialize the costs—citizens pay for it—and privatize the profits—oligarchs get rich. The U.S. had to leave Afghanistan because this laundromat was no longer profitable. The fighting had slowed to a trickle, and the only people making money were the Afghans on the U.S. payroll, and a few guys doing some drug and human trafficking—that stuff happens in every war. Opium is less important today, now that they have fentanyl, and Ukraine has industrial scale drug labs. The oligarchs knew they were provoking a proxy war against Russia in Ukraine, and there were signs that fighting would begin soon, so they shifted their attention to this more profitable enterprise. The more intense the combat, the higher the profits. Ukraine was already yielding big profits because the U.S. had been arming Ukraine for the last eight years to get them ready to join NATO. The war in Ukraine has turned out to be a massive economic boom for the oligarchs and their laundromat associates in Washington D.C. Senators and Congress members are frothing at the mouth demanding more money for freedom and democracy. The military enterprises in Afghanistan and Iraq were also hugely successful, especially the no-bid Haliburton contracts. The American war against Vietnam was a very profitable enterprise, even though the Vatican lost a reliable slave colony. President Johnson and General Westmoreland got filthy rich from Vietnam. All U.S. wars are successful. General Smedley Butler, a WWI veteran, wrote a short book titled *WAR IS A RACKET*, which will always be relevant. It can be read in one afternoon. Marine Corps veterans are the only people who know who Smedley Butler was because he has been largely erased from history. He was the most highly decorated soldier in U.S. history at the time he wrote his book. The Pentagon is an equal opportunity institution. They obey their masters and delete anyone without regard to race or religion.

To avoid taxes and regulations, and maximize profits, the oligarchs moved manufacturing out of the U.S. to lower cost nations like Mexico, China and Vietnam. While the U.S. shifted to a service economy (banks, retail, coffee shops), Russia and China invested in heavy manufacturing. The U.S. no longer has the industrial base necessary to support a war against a peer military.

Russia and China are not third-world nations. They are highly sophisticated and industrialized societies that have the world's best air defense systems. The Russian and Chinese MICs are purpose-driven. They have large networks of state-owned MICs that directly serve military interests. They don't care about MIC profits, and the MIC doesn't corrupt the government with campaign contributions. They use their MIC to prepare for high-intensity conflicts along their vast borders. The Russians have a capable blue-water navy with a fleet of advanced submarines. They have hypersonic missiles that are highly accurate and cannot be stopped. They have an endless supply of drones. They have about 1,700 ballistic missiles with nuclear warheads. They have large arrays of military satellites for reconnaissance and targeting. They have satellites that can hunt and delete enemy satellites. This is not the military Russia had in 1991, and it's not what the Pentagon planned for.

The CW oligarchs then shifted their focus to Diversity, Equity, and Inclusion (DEI) and Environmental, Social and Governance (ESG) requirements for companies that want to be traded on the stock exchanges. The goal of these initiatives is to advance the authoritarian agenda and consolidate economic control. During this time, Russia and China invested in large infrastructure projects and national defense.

The World Economic Forum (WEF) is where the oligarchs host meetings with middle managers in Davos, Switzerland. Some of the ruling families like to host their own planning conferences. The Club of Rome began in 1970. The Bilderberg Meeting was established in 1954, and was chaired by Prince Bernhard of Lippe until 1975. Prince Bernhard was an SS officer and member of the NATS party during WWII. After the war, aided by the CIA and the Vatican, most of the important NATS escaped prosecution, and were able to keep their wealth. These globalist organizations have the same agenda: Humanity is in a terrible state of affairs, and something must be done to improve this situation to make the world a better place. The globalists are the cause of most of the world's problems, but this is never discussed. The WEF was founded by Klaus Schwab in 1971. He was Henry Kissinger's student. The WEF is not a legislative body. It does not have an army. They are a private NGO whose members have immunity from prosecution. They are greed driven. They are a system of self-enrichment and corruption. They are part of the world revolutionary movement. They are a Fascist-Marxist hybrid, like the governments they represent, who promote authoritarianism. Fascist means that the means of production are privately owned by the oligarchs who control the government. Marxist means the oligarchs employ revolutionaries, who use revolutionary tactics to achieve desired results (order out of chaos). They believe they can recreate the world according to their principles. I have watched video clips from WEF meetings. There were a lot of children and grandchildren of WWII German and Ukrainian NATS in attendance, and they speak English with a heavy German accent. Alex Soros looked terrible, as if he hadn't slept for days. He's American, but I can't understand what he says because he speaks rambling, incoherent gibberish. The WEF features a Young Global Leaders training program in which promising young, rising stars are invited to attend lectures from Professor Klaus on how to be an effective globalist puppet authoritarian leader. Justin Trudeau and Macron are the star pupils. Some of the goals of the WEF are as follows: abolish property rights; abolish fossil fuels; control and constrain the food supply; transform the housing market from owning to renting, and digitize everything. Implementing a global central bank digital currency (CBDC) is critical to population control. The central banks have always promoted totalitarianism and war. All humans will be forced to accept digital currency. In a 2024 speech at Davos, Antonio Guterres, Secretary-General of the United Nations, said, "We can't build a future for our grandchildren with a system that was built for our grandparents. We must have digital passports and digital currency." It sounds so good when it's all about the children.

One of the WEF's major goals is to create a system that will track every individual's carbon dioxide footprint. Humans will be taxed for breathing. Climate change is a complex religion, but whatever one chooses to believe about it, it should be obvious to anyone that it is being used for population control, and diverting public funds into the climate change laundromats. It's amazing that people believe corrupt politicians, un-elected technocrats and oligarchs have the ability to influence Earth's climate, or that giving them more money and power will somehow lead to something positive for society.

When I was in the tenth grade, I learned about photosynthesis, which is the biochemical process green plants use to convert carbon dioxide, water and sunlight into sugar. By following the science, I learned that carbon dioxide is an essential nutrient required for life on Earth. But the globalist climate experts tell us that carbon dioxide is a poisonous gas that causes climate change. Atmospheric carbon dioxide levels are currently around 420 parts per million, or 0.042 percent, which is 50 percent higher than before the industrial revolution. All this extra carbon dioxide is causing plants to grow faster. I have to mow my grass more often. Global food productivity is increasing and food prices are decreasing, outside of the U.S. and EU. Fertilizer prices are decreasing because farmers don't need to use as much. It appears that carbon dioxide is a constraining or limiting micronutrient for green plants. The most significant factors affecting climate are precession of the equinoxes and sun spot activity, but it is forbidden to discuss any natural phenomena in relation to climate. Is it possible that volcanoes below the ice in the Arctic circle might cause some of this ice to melt? That is not possible. Anyone who suggests a natural explanation for any climate phenomenon is shouted down, accused of being a climate science denier, and cancelled. The earth's climate has been in a continual state of change since the earth was formed, and the only people who dispute this scientific fact are the climate alarmist industry. According to them, the earth's climate began to change after the industrial revolution. If they would follow the science, they might learn that droughts, floods, forest fires, hurricanes, glaciers, and tornadoes having been coming and going on this planet since before humans. The politicians who take donations from the climate change industry can't tax nature or G*d, so they target human activity. Climate science is a political science. It is not a natural science.

The new and improved world management system will not feature concentration camps, at least not above ground. We don't know what goes on in deep underground military bases. The resources necessary to sustain human life—water, food, housing and energy—are being bought up by the oligarchs. In order to save the environment, once-productive farms, will lie fallow. Forests will be cut down, and the trees buried in the ground so that humans can't use the wood. Farmers are being forced out of business. Groundwater aquifers will be inaccessible for human use. Surface water sources are already poisoned. The human population will be starved in place, or at least constrained from further growth. Because the EU countries are now sourcing food from lower cost South America, the oligarchs no longer need European farmers. They want to pay the farmers a little money for their land, and make a fortune with new real estate developments. The American farmers and cattle producers are also being forced out of business. Say goodbye to food security. Stalin deleted millions of Ukrainians during the Holodomor in the 1930s by stealing the food they grew. The U.S. government hired frontiersmen to eliminate the bison in order to starve the indigenous people. Pal*stinians are being denied food and water in Gaza. The Israelis launched three drone attacks to delete seven aid workers who were feeding Pal*stinians. Starving humans in place is not a new idea.

According to our globalist rulers, our uncontrolled and irresponsible breeding has caused this resource scarcity, and this is all our fault (gas-lighting). Fortunately, the intellectual elites at Davos are prepared to make the necessary decisions to save the planet, delete the disobedient humans, and steal everything.

Jamie Dimon, the CEO of JP Morgan, said that "governments, business and non-governmental organizations may need to invoke eminent domain in order to get the adequate investments fast enough for grid solar, wind and pipeline initiatives." Mussolini was the first to introduce the business model of public-private partnerships—socialized costs and privatized profits. Fascism is an authoritarian political ideology characterized by a dictatorial leader; centralized autocracy; militarism; forcible suppression of opposition; belief in a natural social hierarchy; subordination of individual interests for the perceived good of the nation or race; and strong regimentation of society and the economy. Fascism is the governance model of the CW, and it describes the WEF.

After the end of WWII, the U.S. government did what it always does, lie about everything. It was actually the Soviets who defeated 80 percent of the German army. About 30 million Soviets perished during WWII. The U.S. and Soviet governments captured as many NATS scientists as fast as they could. About 1,600 NATS scientists and intelligence agents were given new passports and immigrated to the U.S. NASA, the U.S. space agency, was founded by NATS scientists led by Werner von Braun, who designed the V2 rocket in Germany. Reinhard Gehlen and his entire spy team were absorbed into the Office of Strategic Services (OSS), which was later renamed the Central Intelligence Agency (CIA). Gehlen also commanded a leave behind SS Waffen unit in Ukraine. Klaus Barbie, nicknamed the Butcher of Lyon, was recruited to teach the Americans interrogation techniques, such as waterboarding. Barbie was later transferred to the Bolivian government, fearing the Isr*elis would find out he was in the U.S. Ninety-seven-year-old Yaroslav Hunka, a veteran Ukrainian SS Waffen soldier, was recently applauded by the Canadian parliament, with Justin Trudeau, Chrystia Freeland and Zelensky applauding this war criminal. The NATS are alive and well. Their children and grandchildren are middle managers and oligarchs who now run many CW governments, NATO, and the WEF.

William Blum wrote an excellent book titled *Rogue State: A Guide to the World's Only Superpower*, and in it he lays out an exhaustive history of CIA activities in nearly every country of the world, with election rigging, bribery, propaganda, manufactured scandals, illegal wiretapping, kidnapping, extortion, arson, bombings, assassinations, coups, invasions, false flag operations, drug trafficking, human trafficking, gun running, espionage, sabotage, etc. Americans like empire. The YouTube documentary series, "History of the CIA," by Eyes Wide Open presents an excellent and well-documented history of CIA collusion with the Vatican, international bankers, N*ZI SS officers, organized crime, occult secret societies, drug traffickers, terr*rists and communist governments.

The oligarchs are building large, luxurious underground survival bunkers. These bunkers likely have armories full of lethal weapons. When our hero special operations soldiers retire from the military, or whatever, most of them get security jobs working for the oligarchs. Some become mercenaries. A few become space aliens. These people follow the money. The oligarchs surround themselves with goons and guns, but we the people shouldn't have firearms, because our lives are worthless and we can't be trusted with lethal self-defense. Perhaps the oligarchs are preparing for the terr*rism they plan to unleash on humanity. They are masters of terr*rism and ethnic cleansing.

# Middle Managers

The president is the leader of a political party, and that's it. He's always a puppet leader who takes orders from the international bankers. Congress is a debating club. Lobbyists work for the oligarchs, and they write the bills. Congress members vote the way the lobbyists tell them to vote. Most Congress members don't even read the bills they vote on. They are all bribed with campaign contributions, or blackmailed with Epstein videos. The U.S. Constitution describes three branches of government. But after WWII, there emerged a fourth branch of government, the permanent state, which exercises power over the other three. The CIA are the middle managers who run the permanent state for the benefit of the oligarchs. The three branches of government enumerated by the Constitution are managing a theater company.

It's important to understand the nature and character of the men who founded the U.S. Doing so provides insight into the present situation. The northeast coast of the U.S. was originally colonized by the Virginia Company, an English trading company chartered in 1606 by King James I. They grew tobacco and harvested timber for export. It was necessary to delete the indigenous people who didn't appreciate having their gardens and forests stolen by pirates. The Virginia Company was modeled after the British East India Company that eventually conquered India, Pakistan, Myanmar, Bangladesh, and Hong Kong. These people were ruthless pirates. At this time, all the European states were engaged in the same activities. They had steel swords, horses and gunpowder. They sailed fleets of pirate ships around the world looking for new lands to conquer and resources to steal. They searched for societies who had Bronze Age military technology like the bow and arrow and spear. European and British cities were filthy and disease ridden. These pirates were survivors of plagues, so they had immune resistance to the diseases they carried. They carried bioweapons on their filthy bodies wherever they went. All the European powers engaged in slavery. In the Americas, they sent ships to Africa to purchase slaves from powerful African tribes who captured people from neighboring tribes. In Asia they enslaved the indigenous people in place. In America, the indigenous people refused to be slaves, so they had to be deleted and replaced with Africans. This idea of replacing noncompliant people is not new.

Throughout recorded history, all civilizations, everywhere in the world, practiced genocide and slavery. *Slav* is the root of the word slavery. Ninth century Vikings who lived near modern Kiev captured Slavic people and sailed them across the Black Sea to modern Turkiye, where they were sold. The Arabs had a preference for slave women with blond hair and blue eyes. The Barbary pirates sailed along the coasts of southern England and captured a million white slaves. When the Arabs conquered north Africa and southern Europe, they took hundreds of thousands of white slaves. Everyone's ancestors were barbarians and slave traders.

A large population of Pilgrims, white Christians, migrated to the northeast coast of America to escape religious persecution in Europe. Establishment historians and preachers often repeat narratives about the founding fathers being Christian. It's not true. George Washington never set foot in a church unless he had a wedding invitation. For many years he rode a horse and stabbed people with his sword. Jefferson was a deist who believed the Articles of Faith were fiction, and he published his own bible. Benjamin Franklin was a member of the Hell Fire Club, and owned a slave auction. John Adams, America's second president, did not own slaves, and he attended a Unitarian church (not Christian). Aaron Burr deleted Alexander Hamilton in a duel in 1804. Most of the founders were plantation owners, with large whiskey stills. Most U.S. presidents were occultists, scoundrels, murderers and thieves, just like today. The founding fathers were English aristocrats, not pilgrims. The American colony bosses were successful for the following reasons: They adopted the same business practices as the British East India company; they adopted property rights; they adopted the Bill of Rights; and they adopted free market entrepreneurship as opposed to the monopoly capitalism (fascism/oligarchy) we have today.

The colony bosses decided they no longer wanted to share their profits with the British royals. After the British fought a Thirty Years'

War in Europe and a seven-year French and Indian War in America, their financial and military power had weakened. The colony bosses needed an army, but all they had to fight with were these pilgrims. So, they developed a plan to get the pilgrims to fight against the British (proxy war). They established the Articles of Confederation and the Bill of Rights, promising fair government and equal rights (bait and switch). The Pilgrims still didn't want to fight (smart). So, the colony bosses staged the Boston Tea Party (false flag) and some other provocations that led to the British soldiers shooting some of the colonists at Lexington and Concord. They printed propaganda in the newspapers, and finally got about 20 percent of the pilgrims stirred up enough to fight. General Washington got his army. After the new Americans defeated their British overlords, the American Freeloaders became much wealthier. The Articles of Confederation were soon replaced with the Constitution, which enabled the gradual erosion of the Bill of Rights.

Nothing can ever justify slavery. It is an evil practiced by evil men. The white bond servants were considered to be human, while the black slaves were dehumanized. They were considered to be less than human, which justified treating them worse than animals. This is a major reason for the grievances of American Blacks—the chickens have come home to roost. The victimization industry race hustlers, poverty pimps, and community organizers make a lot of money on this grift. This is not going away, not ever. Slavery in the U.S. was deregulated, but not abolished. They moved from a system where the slave master pays for the food, shelter, clothing and medicine, to a system where the wage slave pays for his own upkeep with what little the slave master gives him. Many of the freed slaves continued to work on the plantations where they were slaves. They became wage slaves, and then debt slaves. This model was so successful, they extended it to coal mines, and then the population at large. There is more slavery today than has ever existed. Now, all Americans are being de-humanized. The oligarchs and middle managers hate middle-class working people because we are considered less than human.

As more European migrants arrived, America grew westward until they reached the Pacific Ocean. They developed an idea called Manifest Destiny, in which white Americans were divinely ordained to conquer the continent of North America. The French and Spaniards were doing the exact same thing, but it was G*d's plan that the new Americans would have the privilege of deleting the indigenous people of North America and enriching themselves from the resources obtained. Next came the idea of the Missionary State, which said that it was G*d's plan for Americans to conquer the world to spread the gospel. Today, the U.S. has about 30 million evangelicals who always want more wars for Jesus. Americans then developed the idea of American Exceptionalism, which says that America is distinctive, unique, or exemplary compared to other nations. The U.S. is both destined and entitled to play a distinct role on the world stage. Today, the Americans call themselves The Indispensable State. This is the idea that the U.S. promotes democracy and freedom, and the entire world must be converted to our way of government and culture. That's why we are good, and they are bad. If the Russians, Arabs, Chinese and Africans won't agree to promote LGBTQ (wedge issue), that means they don't share our democratic values. They might need a military intervention as a reform measure. We will take their mineral resources because they don't respect human rights, and we can do a better job of managing them to save the planet and feed the laundromat.

The CW middle managers typically have law degrees, which is the perfect education for a career criminal. An education in drama, or acting, is perfect for someone whose primary job is to read scripts, tell lies, and pretend to be someone they aren't (Trudeau, Macron, Zelensky). Most of them grew up in privileged families, so they have degrees in political science, history, literature, and drama. Few to none have served in their nation's military. They grew up in a culture where rich kids don't work for anything. Everything in life was given to them.

Russian middle managers typically have PhDs in engineering, science, economics, political science, and/or military science. They are hard-working, no non-sense people. Nothing is given to them. They have all served in the military. Vladimir Putin grew up in poverty. He earned his first academic degree in international law from Leningrad State University, and then a PhD in economics. He served many years as an intelligence officer. He is fluent in German and English. He is not a middle manager, even though his official title is president. He is not an oligarch. He owns high value assets, but not a business or factory. He is not a czar—when he leaves office, his children will not inherit his position. He was elected five times, winning 87 percent in the most recent election. The communist party was second with 4 percent of the vote. He is not a dictator. Not even close. I could never pretend to understand Russian politics, but they have an efficient system of checks and balances, and they are a stable society. The Duma is the legislative body. There are the Russian generals, many cabinet departments, the intel guys, the oligarchs, and the Russian Orthodox Church. Before Mr. Putin announces new legislation, he goes through a process of talking to all these people, and getting their support. He spends a lot of time on the phone. The Russian middle managers like to be consulted, and they like for everyone to get along. Mr. Putin works hard to get along with these hard people. In Putin's Russia, the president tells the oligarchs what to do. After the fall of the Soviet Union, Mr. Putin's predecessors were giving the country away and letting the oligarchs purchase state assets for a fraction of their value. The CW countries were happy with this resource stealing arrangement. When Putin seized power, he stopped the stealing, and instituted reforms that angered the U.S. Putin brought law and order back to Russia, and made his nation a powerful empire once again.

The CW middle managers hate Putin because they are jealous. He is the leader of a powerful sovereign empire in ascendancy, and he is loved by the Russian people. The CW middle managers are puppets and script readers for states that are ruled by oligarchs, are becoming less relevant, and are collapsing domestically under poor leadership. Putin is the most respected world leader in history. They are hated by their citizens and mocked daily. Putin earned a judo black belt, and can put a big man on the floor in three seconds. They play golf. Putin is intelligent and sophisticated. Joe Biden is a heavily medicated, senile old gangster who can barely walk, and has to have his diaper changed—sympathies to the Secret Service agent assigned that duty. Mr. Putin sometimes shares his wit and humor with the press. On the subject of Burkina Faso, Putin told the French President, "The vampire ball is over. You got your bellies full of human flesh, and your pockets stuffed full of money, and now it's time to go." That is hilarious.

The western psyche developed from a peculiar history and culture. The CW middle managers are uncivilized and violent. They are morally unsophisticated. They are morally and intellectually undeveloped. They hate peace, because they love war profiteering. They have a culture that glorifies gangsters, cowboys and tough guys. They believe in conquest, exploitation, domination, and subjugation. They promote a hierarchy of cruelty, where everyone uses and abuses everyone else of lower status. They do not negotiate or compromise. They don't believe in fair and harmonious transactions. They are the best, so they can do what they want. Because they can do what they want, they are the best. They believe in the last man standing. Everything is ours and nothing is yours. Capitalism means we make the money at someone else's expense. This is their approach to the world. They dehumanize anyone who has anything they want to steal. African slaves were dehumanized for their labor. The Vietnamese were dehumanized because they wanted freedom from slavery and religious persecution. Now the CW are dehumanizing their own populations. These middle managers have no regard for human life. Their actions are justified by the fact that they can do them. They have no appreciation for the gravity of violence or its consequences. They are offended by any constraints on their belligerence. The entire world should subordinate themselves and offer them tribute. They are barbarians and pirates. They pretend they are good, enlightened and virtuous people, and they attack anyone who questions their authority or virtue.

Manufacturing in the U.S. has declined considerably since the Eisenhower administration. The U.S. has betrayed anyone who might be their ally or proxy partner. Biden promised he would destroy the Nord Stream pipeline. This was the largest act of ecoterr*rism and political betrayal in history. This is how the U.S. treats its German colony. The U.S., Britain, Germany, and France are collapsing under the weight of self-enrichment and corruption. They can no longer compete in global markets. They have been left behind. They are facing rock bottom, and they are in denial. They are a rabid dog menacing the global neighborhood.

It looks like France might lose some of its remaining colonies. The Africans have made security agreements with Russia, and they told the French and the U.S. to please leave and take their hired ISIS terrorists with them. France enslaved these countries with unfair mining deals and French fiat currency. French Africa, fourteen African nations enslaved under French colonial rule, existed from 1895 to 1958. Why are these resource-rich nations so poor? Maybe Mr. Macron and his vampire friends would know the answer. Let's wish the Africans well in their future endeavors, and hope the people there can achieve a better life. The Africans should look to Vietnam as an example of a nation that endured slavery and war for over one hundred years, but then rose from the ashes like a phoenix.

The sanctions have forced Russia and China into an alliance, and made them stronger. Sanctions compel decision makers to find new supply sources and new ways of doing business. Chinese chip makers are better off now. U.S. curbs on chip exports forced China to improve their own chip making capabilities. China is currently manufacturing 3 nm chips. They estimate in three years they will be manufacturing photon chips that will make all other microchips obsolete due to efficiency improvements. Sanctions create new markets and business methods.

The U.S. has forced the fascist European states to re-arm and once again become a belligerent military menace. Russia and China have limitless supplies of cheap energy, required for an advanced industrialized society. The CW is pursuing an economy based on windmills and solar panels. Those windmills look good on the cover of an annual report. The energy corporations get ESG points for that, and the executives get their ESG bonuses. Together, Russia and China are self-sufficient and self-sustaining. They no longer need or want anything from the CW. Being isolated from the CW is the best thing that could happen to a nation. It's like breaking up with a crazy feminist. No one enjoys watching the U.S. destroy itself, but this might be the only path to peace, prosperity and security for the rest of the world.

The sanctions against Russia and China are destroying the economies of the CW. The middle managers don't seem to understand fundamental economic principles. The Europeans have purposely diminished their supply of inexpensive energy from Russia. Europeans prefer to pay higher prices for refined petroleum products from India.

They prefer to pay four times the price for American Liquified Natural Gas (LNG). Higher energy costs increase the price of goods and services. Higher energy costs always increase price inflation. In response to increased price inflation, caused by higher energy costs, caused by the sanctions, the CW managers raised interest rates, which increased inflation even more. *Price inflation* is the rate of increase in prices over a given period of time. It is the increase in the cost of living in a country. Increasing interest rates increases the borrowing cost for consumers, so that mortgages, auto loans and credit card debt become more expensive. Increasing interest rates increases the cost of living for consumers. Increasing interest rates increases inflation. The octogenarian economic experts tell us they must raise interest rates in order to reduce inflation. This is a big lie. As inflation climbs higher, they keep increasing interest rates and forcing price inflation even higher. The U.S. government and media are intentionally deceiving an economically ignorant public. They are intentionally increasing inflation and collapsing the housing market. One of their goals is for home owners to become renters and homeless people.

Home and auto insurance rates are skyrocketing. Credit card debt and payment delinquencies are increasing. Consumers have stopped paying credit card debt, student loans and car payments. U.S. consumers are borrowing against their 401K retirement accounts and applying for home equity loans.

The Federal Reserve Bank is a privately owned bank. The international bankers create money from nothing and loan it to the U.S. Treasury, with interest and conditions. *Monetary inflation* occurs when the Federal Reserve creates more currency. Actually, they just add numbers to the public debt on an accounting ledger in an Excel spreadsheet. As the supply of money increases, the value of the currency decreases, which means that consumers have to spend more money to get the same amount of goods. The money supply has to be inflated so that the government can spend more. Government spending and money creation is what causes increased inflation. Government spending and stock buybacks are keeping stock prices inflated, which creates the illusion that the economy is growing.

The Federal Reserve Bank was created by a congressional act in 1913. Woodrow Wilson signed the act into law because he was being threatened with a sex scandal. 1n 1919, Wilson said,

"I am a most unhappy man. I have unwittingly ruined my country. A great industrial nation is now controlled by its system of credit. We are no longer a government by free opinion, no longer a government by conviction and the vote of the majority, but a government by the opinion and duress of a small group of men."

The American economy is not growing. Workers are being fired. Businesses are closing. Small businesses can't pay their rent. Thousands of retail stores are closing due to massive looting by the entitlement class. Demand for freight services is weakening. Logistics companies are losing money. Business inventory is down. Consumer spending is decreasing. Manufacturing long ago moved to China and Mexico. Government spending is 80 percent of the U.S. gross domestic product (GDP). For the first quarter of 2024, GDP was 1.6 percent. This is not a hot economy. Joe Biden has repeatedly said this is the greatest economy in American history. He says that American attitudes are the problem. It's all a problem of public perception. Lying and gas lighting are Biden's favorite communication devices.

When economic growth increases, more money flows into the market, which increases inflation. Economic growth can be tamped down by increasing interest rates, which causes businesses to borrow less and curtail new projects or expansion. But there is no economic growth in the U.S. The so-called bull market was caused by stimulus spending during the stage-managed epidemic. If the U.S. oligarchs wanted to decrease inflation, they would lower government spending, lower energy prices and lower interest rates. They are doing the exact opposite. The American consumer, being a product of the American education system, is too ignorant to understand fundamental economic principles. The consumer just knows that his adjustable-rate mortgage, his car payment, his credit card bill, food prices, and his entire cost of living is increasing with increasing interest rates, energy sanctions, and reckless government spending.

*Monetary inflation* is caused by growing the money supply. The one huge asset bubble causing inflation is the U.S. dollar. Deficit spending causes inflation because it floods the market with newly created money. China has been aggressively selling U.S. Treasury bonds. Japan was also forced to sell U.S. Treasury bonds in order to prop up the falling yen. All nations, outside the CW, are selling U.S. Treasury bonds.

Biden's economic adviser is Jared Bernstein, who promotes Modern Monetary Theory (MMT), which is the largest financial scam in world history. The premise is that deficit spending is good for the economy, as long as the money is being used for good things like stimulus spending and climate change. The MMT experts tell us that deficit spending is always good for someone. It is definitely good for the oligarchs. When Mr. Bernstein explains MMT, he uses vague and confusing language to hide the truth about who exactly issues the U.S. currency. The U.S. federal government is not the issuer of U.S. currency. At the top of every paper bill are printed the words Federal Reserve Note. In order to pay for more laundromat spending, the U.S. Treasury must issue bonds, which are then purchased with dollars created by the Federal Reserve. This new money is then used to buy more corruption. What Mr. Bernstein is hiding is the fact that the Federal Reserve is a private bank owned by his oligarch friends, who pocket the interest payments.

Interest payments do not go into the U.S. Treasury, as falsely claimed for the last hundred years. Interest on debt, currently at $1.2 trillion, is now the largest expenditure in the federal budget. Continued money printing is unsustainable. The Federal Reserve must keep interest rates high in order to prop up bond rates. At this point, the only way to avoid a sovereign debt crisis is to raise taxes, and Biden has said that a $5 trillion tax increase is coming. Every U.S. president always out-spends the previous administration. If the U.S. government can simply print the money it needs, then why do they have to borrow money by printing bonds? A better question to ask is: Why can't the U.S. get rid of the Federal Reserve Bank? Representative Thomas Massie has symbolically introduced HR 8421, the Federal Reserve Board Abolition Act. A similar bill was introduced by Ron Paul, and likewise ignored.

A large number of Treasury bonds held by China have reached maturity. The U.S. dollars received by China for the expired bonds are then used to purchase gold from the U.S. Commodities Exchange. The Chinese take physical delivery of the gold in Hong Kong. Going forward, the non-aligned states will be reluctant to buy U.S. Treasury bonds at any rate.

The CW managers have weaponized the U.S. dollar, which for decades has been the major source of U.S. power. They decided to steal Russia's international foreign trade reserves. Now, the rest of the world no longer wants to trade with U.S. dollars because the CW can just steal it when it sits in their banks. The rest of the world is running to BRICS. BRICS+ is a monetary and trade partnership that includes Brazil, Russia, India, China, and South Africa. Several other nations have joined, and another fifty nations are in the process of joining. Soon, the CW states will be the only ones enslaved to the dollar. The U.S. government destroyed the monetary system that gave them power. They cooked and ate the goose that laid the golden eggs.

Joe Biden promised to destroy the fossil fuel industry. Shutting down the Keystone pipeline and blowing up the Nord Stream pipeline was a good start. Germany built windmills and closed their nuclear power plants. The resulting EU economy is in tatters. Perhaps the EU Commission should fire Ursula von der Leyen and replace her with Greta Thunberg. It's not an elected position, and Greta might do a better job as EU president. Greta is the climate change actress who dropped out of high school.

George Bush Jr. cancelled the Anti-Ballistic Missile Treaty (ABM), and Trump cancelled the Intermediate-Range Nuclear Forces Treaty (INF). Russia's response to this stupidity was to build better missiles. Russia realized the U.S. had no interest in missile diplomacy and was constantly seeking ways for unilateral dominance. The U.S. installed missile bases in its NATO colonies, and told the Russians they were targeting Iran, which was a lie. They told the Russians these missiles were not nuclear capable, which was another lie. This situation isn't good for the average American, who doesn't have a bomb shelter. The CW oligarchs and their middle managers have decided that nuclear confrontation with Russia and China is survivable, for them. It appears the CW wants nuclear war.

Russia has vast mineral resources estimated at $100 trillion USD. With inflation, its value is probably ten times that. The CW pirates and bankers have been trying to plunder this wealth for the last 200 years, and they are willing to fight to the last Ukrainian white man to get it. In the YouTube video "*Quiet Part Out Loud: Linsey Graham Drools Over Ukraine Minerals,*" by Breaking Points, June 2024, U.S. Senator Graham said that the trillions in mineral wealth are a major reason for this war. The CW middle managers are desperate. They think Russia's mineral wealth will save their dying economies, and they want to expand their laundromat enterprises.

One of the tactics they use, successfully in Ukraine, to loot a country is to appoint a government in exile, and then work to overthrow the democratically elected government currently in power. The man they chose to be their hero in Russia was Alexi Navalny. He was a small-time embezzler who cheated his business associates in some timber deals. He became a western intelligence asset, working for both MI6 and CIA, and the Russians monitored his activities. The U.S. invested tens of millions into this man's efforts to be a political opposition leader who would get Putin voted out of office, and bring freedom and democracy to Russia, which means they want a gay pride parade in downtown Moscow. At his peak, Navalny could get votes from maybe two percent of Russia's liberal population in Moscow and Leningrad. They all left the country in 2022 to avoid military conscription. Navalny was an idiot drug addict and a racist who hated M*slims and committed violence against them. The M*slim population in the Russian Federation is about 20 percent. The businessmen whom Navalny cheated, made a fuss and pressured the Russian government to prosecute him. Previous to this, the Russians told Navalny he was free to go live in America with his family and his intel sponsors. But the CIA would not allow Navalny to leave Russia because they had so much invested in him. He made a devil's bargain, and he stayed in Russia. The Russians prosecuted him for his financial crimes and sent him to prison where he died from longstanding health problems. He was never a political threat to Putin, or anyone, and they didn't think or care much about him. In an interview after his most recent election victory, Putin said his intel guys tried to make a prisoner swap, on the condition that Navalny could never return to Russia. The CIA didn't want Navalny. He was of no use to them outside of Russia. He was a traitor and small-time crook who died in jail. His children will be given well-paying careers in the U.S. media or State Department, and the coup program against Russia will continue.

Yuri Bezmenov was a Soviet journalist stationed in New Delhi, India, who reported on KGB activities. In 1970, he defected to the United States and was re-settled in Canada. In 1983, his interview on the *David Frost Show* was seen by millions, and has been seen by many more millions on YouTube since then. He described the four stages of conquest used by the Soviets in Eastern Europe, and he said the Soviets were performing clandestine operations in the U.S., which was not true. He told the U.S. State Department that he was a KGB agent, which was not true, and he got away with it. He was a very effective liar. Jack Barsky, who was one of two KGB agents captured inside the U.S., gave an interview on the Patrick Bet-David podcast in 2022, *"Former KGB Spy Reveal's Russia's Plan to Bring America Down."* Mr. Barsky was promoting his book, *Deep Undercover: My Secret Life and Tangled Allegiances as a KGB Spy in America.* Jack said that Yuri was a fake who just wanted to live in America. I believed Yuri's stories for many years. Most of the things he talked about were true. He was living in India when the Beatles and all their hippy friends were visiting a fake laundromat guru in the hills. Yuri was an intelligent and knowledgeable man, and he pursued the greener grass. Russia has never had the ability or desire to invade the U.S., but Hollywood will continue making propaganda films about Russian armies invading America (fear porn). Barsky said that one of the KGB's greatest accomplishments was a propaganda smear campaign against J. Edgar Hoover, in which the KGB successfully planted a story that Hoover was a cross dresser. Hoover actually was a cross dresser who participated in homosexual orgies, which he hid from the public. His close friends called him "Mary."

Obama, and then Trump, and now Biden (bi-partisan sandwich), failed to remove Syrian President Bashar al-Assad, who is loved by his people, but they have been successful at stealing the country's resources. To destabilize the Syrian government, the Obama gang invented the Islamic State of Iraq and Syria (ISIS). They funded and armed Sunni Islamic terr*rists to wage war against the Syrian government. They re-branded and refitted Al-Qaeda for a different conflict. ISIS are terr*rists for hire. They are mercenaries who worship money and pretend to be M*slims. They also hire out for laundromat conflicts in Africa. ISIS have never attacked Israel, and many wounded ISIS terr*rists have been treated at Isr*eli hospitals. Currently about 2,000 U.S. troops are illegally occupying eastern Syria, where the oil deposits are located. These U.S. troops have an Airborne Warning and Control System (AWACS) plane flying overhead twenty-four hours a day, and they have air defense, so it's not easy to dislodge them. They are sitting ducks being used as a tripwire. This is the region of Syria where wheat and other crops are grown. Before the U.S. invasion, these crops were used to feed the Syrian people. Evangelicals love it when M*slims are starved and deleted. Trump said, "We're keeping the oil. We have the oil. The oil is secure. We left troops behind only for the oil." It's interesting how well the two political parties work together when the oligarchs want them to. Trump boldly proclaimed that he would eliminate ISIS, so he reduced their funding. The U.S. impoverishes and collectively punishes the Syrian people over a CIA fake media story. This is all about an oil pipeline the Syrian government doesn't want. Bashar al Assad will not subordinate his country and pay the required tribute. The Russians have been sending ship loads of wheat to feed the Syrian people. The Russians had military bases in Syria long before the U.S. The Russians are in Syria by invitation of the democratically elected government. The U.S. military is an invading and occupying imperial power, stealing a poor countries' resources. Syria had democracy and Christianity long before the U.S.

On October 8, 2023, Joe Biden said he would immediately send

$1 billion to the Isr*elis and $100 million to Hamas. There shouldn't be any confusion about who funds Hamas. Biden said it on live TV. The conflict in Isr*el is a massive deception. This is a business deal that supports a lot of laundromat activity. There are weapons transfers, and there is the endless humanitarian assistance grift inside the United Nations Relief and Works Agency (UNRWA). Yasser Arafat, head of the Palestinian Liberation Organization (PLO), was a Freeloader, and so is Mahmoud Abbas, the current leader of Hamas. Hamas and the PLO were founded in Cairo, Egypt, by the Musl*m Brotherhood, which is Freem*sonry for M*slims only. Recep Tayyip Erdogan, until recently the president of Turkiye, is the grand potentate of the Musl*m Brotherhood. The headquarters for Hamas are in Qatar. The Hamas leadership team are billionaires who live in mansions and fly around in private jets. Muammar Gaddafi, the Libyan prime minister from 1969 to 2011, who was murdered by an Obama proxy, confirmed that the billionaire Arafat was a Freem*son.

Both sides of the negotiations for the two-state solution were always Freem*sons. There was never going to be a Palst*inian state. Arafat was a paid stooge. Jimmy Carter and Bill Clinton are scoundrels for orchestrating this two-state charade. This entire enterprise is a perpetual grift. Occupation leads to resistance which leads to more occupation. M*rder leads to revenge m*rder which leads to more m*rder. The circle of money goes round and round, just like a washing machine. It's okay if people don't like Islam, but this level of m*rder and cruelty isn't necessary, and it transforms Israel and the U.S. into more barbaric societies. Whatever good will or respect the rest of the world had for these two terr*rist states is gone. The Isra*lis do whatever they want to do because they can. They control a large number of U.S. politicians with campaign contributions and blackmail. Some U.S. weapons transferred to black markets in Ukraine are now in the Middle East and Mexico. The Bronze Age people now have tools like the Raytheon Javelin, shoulder-fired anti-tank missile. Trump liked to brag about all those "tank busters" he was sending to Ukraine. He bragged that all Obama would give them was helmets, but he was sending them the good stuff. Now international terr*rists and Mexican drug cartels have these tank busters. Hopefully, Americans will remember this the next time a passenger jet is shot down. Pal*stinian political elections are very similar to U.S. elections. The Pal*stinian people can vote for the Hamas Freem*son or the PLO Freem*son candidate. The political candidates are chosen by the M*slim Brotherhood, and any opposing candidates are kept in Isr*eli prisons. No matter the election result, the Pal*stinians always vote for a terr*rist entity that serves Israel. The U.S. evangelicals wag their fingers and say, those Pal*stinians always vote for a terr*rist. A political calculation has been made: The Pal*stinians must be starved and deleted. As shown in the YouTube video titled *"Lindsey Graham Calls for Nuking Gaza in Zionist Rant,"* from Richard Medhurst, May 2024, this South Carolina senator wants to use nuclear weapons on unarmed Pal*stinian civilians. We the people have elected this psychopathic lunatic four times. Hopefully, Americans will remember this the next time America is attacked by "extremists." The M*slims aren't angry because Americans have freedom. The Musl*ms are angry because the U.S. government will not stop the endless bombing and terr*r campaigns against Islamic people. For the Isr*elis and their evangelical associates, there are no Pal*stinians. There is only Hamas. Hamas is hiding in every building, car, school, grocery store, hospital, and water pipe. The Isr*elis are not fighting an army, they just bomb everything. The Isr*elis occasionally stumble into an ambush, and they turn around and run away.

In his 2020 state of the union address, Trump announced that the U.S. government had appointed Juan Guaido to be the new president of Venezuela. They appointed an entire government in exile for another nation, without consulting the democratically elected leadership of Venezuela. The United Nations (UN) quietly approves of the U.S. government appointing leaders for other nations. The UN quietly approves of anything the U.S. and Isr*eli governments do. This is what is meant by the "international rules-based order." The CIA makes the rules, and everybody else better fall in line. This is bipartisan. Nancy Pelosi and every Congress member gave a standing ovation. Trump had previously attempted a failed paramilitary coup to steal Venezuela's oil. Guaido is hated by the Venezuelan people. He is a traitor and a con man. He was run out of the country, and currently lives a luxurious lifestyle in Miami at U.S. government expense. This pattern has been repeated all over the world.

Imran Khan was the prime minister of Pakistan from 2018 to 2022. Pakistan has always had good trade and diplomatic relationships with Russia and China. It's called getting along with one's neighbors. But the neighborhood bully lives 10,000 miles away in Washington DC. The previous bully was 6,000 kilometers away in Britain. Pakistan needs money from foreign trade. After the Ukraine enterprise began, Imran Khan was told to join the sanctions movement against Russia and declare Putin to be a war criminal. In November 2022 Khan was shot in an attempted assassination. In January 2024 he was found guilty in a corruption case and sentenced to 14 years. Khan got the Trump treatment, except that Trump hasn't been shot yet. Mr. Khan was a famous cricket player, and he is very popular with the voters. Pakistan is not a sovereign nation, and the smallest disobedience must be severely punished. There aren't many sovereign nations left in the world: Russia, China, Iran, India, North Korea, Saudi Arabia, Vietnam, and Cuba. These are the axis of evil nations.

India Minister of External Affairs Jaishankar told U.S. Secretary of State Antony Blinken that India will exercise their options in their relationship with Russia. India needs money, so they refine Russian oil, and sell it to the EU states with a nice mark up. The U.S. bully is angry. The CW did not consult India before they placed sanctions on Russian oil. India was invaded by the British East India Company, and from 1858 to 1947 they were a British colony. India has had good relations with Russia ever since they gained independence from British slavery. India will not betray an old friend, or sacrifice their own economy just because Joe Biden's son took bribes from Ukraine. India appears to be a sovereign nation, and the U.S. doesn't tolerate that. In April 2024, India announced they would stop buying Russian oil "delivered on Sovcomflot tankers." They continue to buy Russian oil delivered by other carriers. Mr. Jaishankar might live a while longer.

# NED and Open Society Foundation

The National Endowment for Democracy (NED) is a regime change organization. It's a Non-Governmental Organization (NGO) funded by the U.S. State Department (oxymoron). The NED promotes the interests of the U.S. intelligence agencies. They create the conditions necessary to advance color revolutions and manufacture wars for profit. The NED organizes and funds programs to destabilize governments on their target list, which includes almost every country in the world. They rig the elections in much of the world. They publish propaganda to educate the world about the deplorable human rights conditions, and lack of freedom and democracy that exist in the countries they target for destabilization and military invasion. They collaborate with dis-enfranchised groups to create political activism.

NED selects children of prominent foreign nationals, and gives them scholarships to Harvard and Yale. They are recruited into a Young Leaders Program and educated by the U.S. State Department on how to be a U.S. puppet leader, a Manchurian candidate. These young acolytes are celebrated, and their egos are puffed up with endless flattery. They are promised great fame and fortune. After they return to their home country, the media creates favorable narratives about their accomplishments and vision to improve the country. Then the NED funds and organizes their political campaigns.

From 2010 to 2012 the NED organized the First Arab Spring in Tunisia, Libya, Egypt, Yemen and Syria. The rulers in Tunisia, Libya, Egypt and Yemen were removed and replaced with U.S. puppet leaders. The NED organized color revolutions in Belarus, Georgia, Ukraine, Kyrgyzstan, and Yugoslavia with the aim of establishing western-style liberal colonies in those countries.

From 2013 to 2014, the NED removed the democratically elected government of Ukraine in a coup, and installed a U.S. client regime. Forty-eight pro-Russian activists were beaten and burned alive in the Trade Unions House in Odessa. The U.S. and NATO built up Ukraine's military to fight a proxy war against Russia. From 2014 to 2022 the Ukraine NATS shelled and deleted 14,000 Russian speaking civilians living in eastern Ukraine. The U.S. and Ukraine provoked this war with Russia.

The British rule in Myanmar lasted from 1824 to 1948. This country has a turbulent and complex history. The British ended the monarchy by sending the royal family into exile, and they separated the government from religious affairs. (Thailand is next.) The British installed a brutal military dictatorship that has ruled the nation since then. Myanmar has many indigenous tribal groups who want to be autonomous or independent, and they have engaged in guerrilla warfare against the central government ever since the British occupation.

Unifying this country was always an impossible challenge.

Aung San was a politician, liberation activist, and revolutionary. He served as Prime Minister of British Burma from 1946 until he was assassinated in 1947. Six months later, Myanmar achieved independence. Aung San is considered the founder of modern Myanmar and the Father of the Nation.

Aung San Suu Kyi is his youngest daughter. In 1968 she worked at the United Nations for three years, married a British MI6 agent and had two children. She was awarded the Nobel Peace Prize in 1991 for her non-violent struggle for democracy and human rights. She served as State Counsellor of Myanmar from 2016 to 2021. She played a vital role in Myanmar's brief transition from military junta to partial democracy in the 2010s. She deserves our admiration and respect.

The military generals have ruled Myanmar since the British left in 1948. They have twice attempted to install a civilian government because they know the government needs reform. One of their problems is that Suu Kyi will always win any election, and she is the only civilian leader the people want. She only has value to the CW intel agencies if she remains in Myanmar as political opposition. The generals will not allow the spouse of a British intel agent to be prime minister. The generals banned her from politics and held her under house arrest for many years. This seventy-eight-year-old woman has been confined to a Myanmar prison since March 2021. This is her reward for her long-standing loyalty to the British and U.S. intelligence agencies.

Myanmar shares a border with China, who is their largest trading partner. China has a petroleum pipeline through the country and many manufacturing facilities and businesses located inside Myanmar. These Chinese businesses create jobs for Myanmar people. Myanmar is a critical partner of China's Belt and Road Initiative, which makes the U.S. feel threatened. The U.S. has a critical national security interest on every square foot of the planet, and all nations must subordinate their interests to the U.S. Because the Myanmar generals don't agree with the "rules-based order," Myanmar is being targeted by the NED for regime change. These two friendly nations who share a border, must not have trade or diplomatic relations, because the U.S. bully doesn't like it when other nations pursue peace and prosperity. The U.S. does nothing for Myanmar other than supply weapons to insurgents.

NED has appointed an opposition government in exile for Myanmar. All members of the National Unity Government (NUG) live in the U.S. The U.S. has been sending weapons to the tribal guerillas through its agents in Thailand, which violates the UN Charter and the rules established by the Association of South East Asian Nations (ASEAN). The guerillas are happy to accept weapons and training from the U.S. government, but they will never recognize the NUG, and they will use these weapons against the NUG when the time comes. The guerillas behave a lot like terrorists, and some of them are opium growers who don't like to share their profits with the Myanmar generals. The Myanmar generals will fight to the last man to keep the CW intel agents out of their government. Not all the Myanmar generals are evil, and the tribal people should live free from violence in their own autonomous regions. China and Russia have had a lot of success governing autonomous regions. There are intelligent and compassionate people in Thailand who could put a stop to this nonsense. Thailand, with its ASEAN partners, could play a more constructive role to help Myanmar maintain their sovereignty, reform the military, and install a civilian government that excludes the NED and other hostile western intel assets. But Thailand is practically a NATO member, so they are only permitted to advance the interests of their CIA bosses. The only outcome acceptable to the U.S. is the military defeat of the Myanmar generals, and the installation of a U.S. government hostile to China.

Thailand is not a sovereign state, and they are under pressure to no longer be a kingdom. Thailand and Myanmar are in the early stages of a developing proxy war against China.

The Rohingya people are Sunni Muslim migrants who moved into Myanmar from Bangladesh. They mostly inhabit Rakhine State, located in western Myanmar. They swam across the Naf River, built bamboo homes, and brought their families across. They have no identification or deeds for the land they squat on. Myanmar does not have birth right citizenship in their legal constitution. The Rohingya culture is incompatible with the Buddhist people who founded Myanmar. Myanmar did nothing to destabilize Bangladesh and cause this migration. During their colonial rule, the British government invited the Muslim Rohingya to live in Buddhist Myanmar. This became a jihad invasion. During WWII, Myanmar was occupied by the Japanese. The Office of Strategic Services (OSS) gave weapons to the Rohingya with the understanding they would use those weapons against the Japanese. The Rohingya did not shoot a single Japanese soldier. Instead, they slaughtered about 20,000 Buddhist people, and burned their temples. Since that time, the Rohingya have been attacking police barracks and stealing weapons. In 2016, the Myanmar generals pushed the million or so Rohingya terrorists and their families back across the river into their country of origin. They didn't leave peaceably. The UN and CW media have been running an intense propaganda campaign against Myanmar ever since. The CW media called Suu Kyi a genocidal war criminal. She wasn't involved with the repatriation, but the media said she was supposed to order the generals to stand down and let the Rohingya return to Myanmar and resume their jihad. The CW doesn't tolerate independent sovereign nations who exercise self-defense against CW proxies. The British government, who created this situation, should send transport planes to Bangladesh and offer refugee asylum status to every one of these million Rohingya Muslims.

The Xinjiang Autonomous Region is the most western Chinese province that borders Pakistan and Tajikistan. It's a huge province that includes the Gobi Desert. It is a critical path for the Belt and Road Initiative (BRI). About 26 million Muslims inhabit Xinjiang, and they are called Uyghurs. From about 1990 to 2010, Uyghur extremists, Sunni Islamic terr*rists, committed thousands of attacks against Chinese people, mostly with knives and axes. They would infiltrate large crowds at markets or train stations and slaughter hundreds of Chinese at a time. In 2010, thousands of Uyghur extremists travelled to Syria to participate in Obama's jihad against Bashar al-Assad. The Chinese government set up road blocks at all entrances into Xinjiang, with the goal of not allowing the Uyghur terr*rists (Obama proxies) to return to the Region. China sent counter terr*rism teams to Syria specifically to hunt and delete these Uyghur terr*rists. Thanks to Obama, the Chinese military gained valuable and much needed battlefield experience, which they were lacking. China began an intense re-education program to teach the Uyghur people employable skills. They arrested extremists by the thousands and put them in prisons where they belong. Since 2010, there haven't been any terr*r attacks. The population of peaceful Uyghurs in Xinjiang is growing. They are now a happy and prosperous region, free of terr*r. In 2023, 260 million tourists visited Xinjiang.

The State Department launched an intense propaganda campaign against China. In her 2022 report, the UN High Commissioner for Human Rights found some instances of "arbitrary and discriminatory detention" (jailing terr*rists), but her report fell short of crimes against humanity or gen*cide. This infuriated the U.S. State Department. The UN Commissioner looked afraid. She will likely be replaced or deleted for this betrayal. But how can there be gen*cide in a population that is happy and well fed, and is growing in numbers?

NED is sponsoring a ring of chaos around China with the goal of disrupting the BRI. They need enough Asian partners to form a coalition of the willing to invade China and rescue the Uyghurs. It's interesting that the Arab world has remained silent on the Uyghur gen*cide myth. It's because they know the truth. People who watch BBC and CNN (lie factories) will never know the truth about anything. The NED is creating another gen*cide myth to justify another money-making invasion. The journalists who are creating this propaganda have never been to Xinjiang, and don't ever intend to go there. The U.S. issued a level 4 advisory against travel to Xinjiang, because they don't want Americans to go there and see the truth.

After a certain Secretary of State ran her government operation on a private server in her home, eighteen Chinese assets disappeared and were never heard from again. Now, no one wants to provide human intelligence and get burned by this reckless and careless U.S. agency. Now, the U.S. must rely on open-source information, and the think tank echo chambers who always tell the naked emperor how beautiful his clothes are.

The Chinese government has been building amazing development projects in Xinjiang. They have salt water lakes that grow seafood abundantly. Their salt water lakes were perfect for salt water fish; they just needed to add some micronutrients, probably iron oxide. They have developed a rice variety that grows in brackish water. They are greening the deserts. They built the world's largest solar energy generation in the desert. China is building the world's first thorium molten salt reactor (TMSR) in the Gobi. China has the world's second largest, behind India, deposits of thorium. TMSR is the safest and most efficient reactor technology ever designed. TMSR was developed at Oak Ridge Tennessee. The Nixon administration ruled against TMSR because it doesn't produce plutonium for weapons. Also, there were some technical issues that Oak Ridge couldn't overcome at that time, which the Chinese have since resolved. Fluoride salts are the most corrosive materials on earth, but the Chinese developed a high nickel stainless steel alloy which solved that problem. Tourists can ride a high-speed train to Xinjiang, because China has completed 40,000 kilometers of high-speed rail. The U.S. has constructed zero kilometers of high-speed rail. The U.S. no longer has the ability to complete infrastructure projects, and the U.S. prioritizes war spending over any other considerations.

The outgoing President of Taiwan, Tsai Ing-Wen, is a NED asset who is doing everything possible to provoke a war with China. Ms. Zin Mar Aung and Min Ko Niang are NED assets being promoted in Myanmar. Maria Ressa is the NED chairperson in the Philippines. Jose Ramos-Horta is a NED asset running for president in Timor-Leste. Pita Limjaroenrat and Sunai Phasuk are NED assets in Thailand. Using their asset Joshua Wong, the NED organized and funded the 2019 violent protests in Hong Kong, which were supervised by U.S. Secretary of State and former CIA Director Mike Pompeo. The list of NED assets in Asia is long. These people follow the money.

The Open Society Foundation (OSF) is funded and managed by George Soros, and now his son Alex. During WWII, George worked for the NATS in Hungary persecuting J*ws. He is a one hundred-year-old billionaire oligarch who made his fortune trading currency swaps, so he is connected to the international banking families. Many analysts think George and his offspring are psychopaths who hate humanity. Karl Marx was a Satanist. Their greatest joy in life is to destroy nations and create human misery and suffering. There is nothing good in this man or his offspring. Mr. Soros is J*wish by birth and atheist by conviction. In every country or society there are institutions that create stability and unity. The goal of the OSF is to rip those institutions to shreds using propaganda, manufactured scandals, lawfare, political violence, staged media events, and a bag full of dirty tricks.

In every society people have differences, but in certain institutions, they find agreement and common purpose. In the U.S., the justice system is the probably the most critical institution that most Americans value. People want to feel safe. They want law and order. They want a system where they can resolve disagreements without violence. They want to live in a society where everyone is treated fairly and lives by the same rules. They want to live in a society where things work. All across the U.S., the OSF has recruited lawyers who are members of the Democratic Socialists of America, and are Marxist operatives. The OSF organizes and funds the political campaigns of these radicals, revolutionaries and grifters. They get elected, because money always wins U.S. elections, and Mr. Soros has plenty of it. These traitors are in the process of destroying the justice system and de-stabilizing the U.S. The district attorneys installed by the OSF, vigorously prosecute political opponents and any white person who owns a gun, while refusing to prosecute dangerous criminals. The U.S. is now the 129th safest country in the world.

# We the People

Ben Franklin said that, "When people discover they can vote themselves money, that is the end of the Republic." Alexis De Tocqueville in his book *Democracy in America* wrote, "The American Republic will endure until the day Congress discovers that it can bribe the public with the public's money." Thomas Jefferson said,

"If the American people ever allow private banks to control the issue of their currency, first by inflation, then by deflation, the banks and corporations that will grow up around them will deprive the people of all property until their children wake up homeless on the continent their fathers conquered … banking establishments are more dangerous than standing armies; and that the principle that spending money to be paid by posterity, under the name of funding, is but swindling futurity on a large scale."

It's difficult to know if Jefferson was making a strategic policy statement or prognostication, or both. Banking scams were already well developed at this time.

The first rule of politics is that we the people always vote for politicians who promise free stuff. In 2024, the U.S. national debt is around $35 trillion and growing by $1 trillion every ninety days. The U.S. middle managers always prioritize war spending above any other consideration. The interest on debt now exceeds military spending. Spending on humans is getting in the way of U.S. national security (global conquest). Too many humans are getting too much free stuff, and causing climate change. A political calculation has been made— something has to be done about these useless humans. Most of us will soon be replaced by artificial intelligence (AI) robots.

In an Oval Office meeting with Republican Congressional members, the weasels were talking about renewing the Patriot Act, and George Bush Jr. said, "Stop throwing the Constitution in my face. It's just a g*d damned piece of paper." In a rare moment, the truth slipped out of this weasel's mouth. I don't think Donald Trump has ever read the founding document—he never talks about it, so it must not be important. Most of the middle managers in the U.S. government are hostile to the Constitution. They view it as an impediment to their authoritarian goals. The founders intended it to be a flexible document, that should be interpreted through the lens of the world revolutionary movement. The founders were in fact revolutionaries. Their hatred of monarchy and church authority goes back to the betrayal of the Templars by King Philip IV of France and Pope Clement in 1307.

In the U.S., civil asset forfeiture is a process in which law enforcement officers take assets from people who are suspected of involvement with crime or illegal activity. If someone is in possession of cash above some arbitrary amount, they are assumed to be criminals, and their property is taken with no due process or evidence of a crime having been committed. No one ever gets their property returned because they have to prove they are not a criminal. How does one prove a negative? In the U.S., everyone outside of the political class is assumed to be a criminal, a terrorist, or a drug trafficker. Almost all criminal court cases are settled by plea bargain. Defendants who don't have the money needed to pay for a defense, must plead guilty to a lesser charge.

Only wealthy gangsters have the money needed to hire an adequate defense. Almost any court case can be bought out by a monied or well-connected criminal. Typically, the judge, the defense attorney and prosecutor are all Freeloaders. Journalists and whistle blowers are routinely murdered and imprisoned by the U.S. government. Anyone who criticizes Joe Biden or protests against this corrupt and authoritarian government is jailed. Joe Biden's political opponents are prosecuted for fictional crimes. The people in one political party have immunity from prosecution, while the people in the other party are prosecuted for fictional crimes that have no victim. There is no equal protection under the law. Illegal migrants and violent criminals are immune from prosecution. The U.S. has become a lawless and authoritarian state.

The U.S. was never a democracy. The Bill of Rights was invented to fool pilgrims into joining a colonial army. The Constitution was created to nullify the Bill of Rights. The sham elections hosted by the two political parties are theatrical productions designed to keep voters believing in the idea of government by and for the people. The people can vote for the R Freeloader or the D Freeloader. Those are the only two choices allowed. U.S. voters are now stuck with a fraudulent, mail-in ballot election system in 28 states, and 35 million migrants registered to vote in sanctuary cities. Election integrity reduces the tendency toward violence. The authoritarians always want more violence. The U.S. has become an ugly and unruly place. The U.S. is and was, from the beginning, a government of, by, and for the oligarchs. As long as the people believe they have representative government, they keep voting for free stuff, and some people get some free stuff. But it's not free—the loans from the oligarchs come with interest and other conditions.

Inside the U.S. House of Congress, on the wall behind the Speaker's podium, on the left and right, are two picture frames, each containing an image of a fasces. This is a symbol of Roman power. This was the symbol of Fascist power used by Mussolini. These fasces are behind the president as he gives the State of the Union address. Fasces was a battle axe with a bundle of rods tied around the axe handle so that it was strong. Why not a bison or a wheat frond? These are American symbols which have been pictured on coins. Symbols are important to the occultists, and they choose them carefully with a purpose. Why is there a pyramid on the back of the one-dollar bill? These are occult symbols. Fascism is the most profitable economic system for monopoly capitalists, in what pretends to be a democratic system of government. The U.S. government wants to be the Fourth Reich, but there's no way these cocaine addicts will last a thousand years.

Patriotic Americans love soldiers and policemen because these people risk their safety for our protection. This makes us feel safe, and we like to feel safe. Americans are told that the U.S. military is defending freedom and democracy. The rest of the world doesn't see it this way. What they see is a foreign aggressor who deletes everybody and steals everything for the oligarchs. What they see is undisciplined violence. In March 1968, 50 soldiers in Charlie Company, raped, clubbed, stabbed and shot to death 500 unarmed villagers at My Lai in South Vietnam. The officers gave unlawful orders. One soldier refused the order to shoot his machine gun at unarmed women and children forced into a ditch. One helicopter pilot called for backup and ended the massacre. This was not a one-time incident. This happened at other villages. This is common behavior in CW militaries. What is uncommon is this one soldier who disobeyed an unlawful order while his Sargent pointed a machine gun at him. U.S. soldiers routinely obey unlawful orders. Julian Assange published videos of the U.S. military deleting some unarmed civilians in Iraq. This is the reason he will spend the remainder of his short life in a U.S. prison. In May 1999, the U.S. bombed the Chinese embassy in Belgrade, eliminating three Chinese journalists. In April 2024, Israel bombed the Iranian embassy in Syria, eliminating seven military advisers. The U.S. and Israel are terr*rist states.

Most U.S. policemen are union members. Their loyalty is to their retirement pension, their union, their lodge, and the middle managers whom they serve. They care nothing about the Constitution or we the people. They will follow an unlawful order every time. If a migrant squatter steals your house, and you don't like it, you will be arrested. If the government doesn't like your speech, you will be arrested. If you exercise your Second Amendment rights, and defend yourself against a violent criminal, you will be arrested. If you think you have rights, a policeman will arrest you and put you in a cage full of queers. I wouldn't call the police under any circumstance. The Fraternal Order of Police Lodge are m*sonic gangsters who work for the middle managers, and no one else. The government pays their salaries, not you.

In April 2007, one mentally ill student at Virginia Tech killed thirty-two people and wounded seventeen others. The police would not go into the building where the shooter was until after he ran out of ammunition and shot himself in the head. Then it was safe for police to enter. There were news camera crews and at least one hundred law enforcement officers assembled outside, but no one would go in. The police strutted and modeled for two hours in front of TV cameras with their pretty black SWAT uniforms and assault gear. In May 2023, almost the same incident happened at Robb Elementary School in Uvalde, Texas. The police strutted around outside in front of the TV cameras and waited for the shooter to run out of ammunition. After nineteen students and two teachers were deleted, and seventeen others wounded, then it was safe for the heroes to go in.

The principal on the money borrowed from the Federal Reserve international bankers is never paid. Every tax-paying American citizen is in debt for the money the middle managers borrow, with interest and conditions, from the oligarchs for the benefit of the oligarchs. What seems to go unnoticed by the public is that private profit schemes are paid for with taxpayer money (socialized costs). The profits from these schemes are paid to the oligarchs (privatized profits). They socialize the costs and privatize the profits. They borrow taxpayer money for war, and then the oligarchs reap the profits from their war factories. They profit on the interest on the money borrowed, and they reap even bigger profits with the business scheme. They get richer while the taxpayer gets poorer. In the past, the ruling class operated on the principle that the rulers need the will of the people, and, using propaganda, they have successfully manipulated the will of the people for over 5,000 years.

The California High-Speed Rail project is a good example of

Governor Newsom's leadership style. Mr. Newsom and his friends just need a lot more money to complete this environmentally challenging project. Ten years from now, they will still need a lot more money, and another ten years. From the perspective of Governor Newsom and his friends, the California High-Speed Rail project has been a huge financial success, for them. In 2023, China completed the 89-mile Jakarta-Bandung high-speed rail in 7 years at a cost of $7.3 billion. Abraham Lincoln built 1,911 miles of railroad in 6 years, and he had to delete indigenous people all the way. The U.S. has constructed zero miles of high-speed rail. Due to corruption and regulations, the U.S. no longer has the ability to complete large infrastructure projects.

Gov. Newsom's administration spent $24 billion to fight homelessness. Now there are 30 thousand more homeless than before, they still have nowhere to live, and no one seems to know what happened to the $24 billion. It disappeared. It's a mystery that has something to do with climate change. Newsom said something about "rain bombs and atmospheric rivers," and how climate change devastated the California economy. There were issues with capital gains, and set aside this and proposition that. This man is a spin doctor, word salad, virtuoso. He's a brilliant liar. California has so many agencies and regulations that all human activity is now a crime. Build Absolutely Nothing Anywhere Near Anything. California is a BANANA republic.

Donald Trump is the best America has to offer. To be fair, he's the only candidate who demonstrates any concern for the welfare of American people, and his team seems better at managing the economy, foreign policy and just about everything else. He stands accused of being a populist. He's good at manipulating crowds, giving campaign speeches, and political brawling. I was disappointed when Trump said that China was a nation of drug addicts. As a product of the U.S. education system, maybe he never heard about the Opium Wars. The

Chinese army went to great lengths to delete the British and American drug traffickers who were shipping opium from India. The Chinese made huge bonfires with the opium they confiscated from the British and American ships. The U.S. is a nation of drug addicts, and Trump blames China for that. He wants to put the homeless drug addicts in tent cities, surrounded by razor wire. He has made a career of blaming China for anything and everything. For over twenty years he has leveled the accusation of currency manipulation, when the U.S. is the world's most malevolent currency manipulator. America's inflation and currency woes are always blamed on others. Trump is a friend to the Federal Reserve Bank and a big supporter of war spending. He takes campaign donations from Big Pharma. He is obedient to the CIA. He is a hyper-Zionist. So, he gets along well with everyone who is important.

In his first term, Trump moved the U.S. embassy to Jerusalem. In his second term, I think the Al-Aqsa Mosque will be replaced with the Third Temple. Make Israel great again. Trump's largest voting bloc are the 30 to 40 million U.S. evangelical Christians. They are Zionist extremists who believe that Jesus will not return until after the Third Temple is built. The design is complete; the stones have been cut; the ritual artifacts have been created; and a small herd of red heifers was recently transported to Israel. Their wish is for Armageddon to occur, so that Jesus will return. The planet must be destroyed, and the disobedient humans must be deleted by war, famine and plagues before Jesus will return. But there is good news. These 30 to 40 million Trump supporters will be spared from the calamities they wish on the rest of us. They will be taken up into the heavenly sky during the Rapture. The Rapture is an idea invented by Zionists which was introduced in 1909 to Americans in the *Scofield Reference Bible*. Cyrus Scofield was a con man preacher who made a business deal with Zionists in New York and the Dallas Theological Seminary to publish a new edition of the Bible.

This is a doomsday cult. In 2018, an Isr*eli organization minted a half shekel coin with Trump's image cast on the front, with the future Third Temple shown on the obverse face. Trump has become a messianic symbol.

In December 2017, Trump commuted the twenty-seven-year sentence of Sholom Mordechai Rubashkin, reducing his sentence by nineteen years. He was the manager of a Kosher meat processing plant near Des Moines, Iowa. He was accidentally arrested by Immigration and Customs Enforcement (ICE) who were investigating the employment of about 600 illegal migrants and minors. ICE found a drug lab and a long list of other crimes, none of which were listed on the search warrant. Rubashkin was charged with bank fraud and tax evasion. Rabbi Rubashkin is a member of the Chabad-Lubavitch Hasidic movement, who are long-time associates of the Trump organization.

Zionism is an international movement originally for the establishment of a J*wish national community in Pal*stine, and later for the support of modern Israel. Before 1948, Pal*stine was home to M*slims, J*ws and Christians. Zionist is not a racial or religious term. There are Christian and J*wish Zionists. There are also Christians and J*ws who are not Zionists. Zionists are people who support removing the people who lived in Pal*stine before 1948 and their descendants, and replacing them with Europeans who call themselves J*ws. After the Holocaust, it was felt that J*ws should be able to do anything they want against non-J*ws.

There are approximately three to four million American Freeloaders who are hyper-Zionists. A Freeloader is someone who wants to serve the J*ws, because they are G*d's chosen people, and G*d doesn't care about anyone else. This is a religion one cannot convert to, unless one has a lot of money. If one can't be a member of the chosenite class, then being a Zionist is the next best thing because God will bless those who bless the chosen people. If you have ever worked in a large company or institution, you might recognize the management style of the Freeloaders—it's managers managing managers, who manage managers, who manage managers, who manage the people who do the work.

Those of us who are not members of the protected class, own nothing. We are allowed to temporarily use the fruits of our labor through titles and deeds, which impart a sense of ownership. If we examine our deeds closely, we might see that we are called the tenant, not the owner. Our children can inherit our tenancy. If we are remiss in paying property taxes, then we may no longer use the property, and our tenancy is revoked. We are always tenants, and never owners. The protected class have ownership deeds. All financial instruments, such as bank deposits, stocks, bonds, etc., are owned by the financial institutions who control them. They collectivize and collateralize our assets to back up their commercial loans and stock market gambling debts. And who do you suppose owns and controls these financial institutions? Schwab owns the stock certificates and bonds, not you. David Rogers Webb wrote *The Great Taking*, which explains the changes made to the banking laws, the Uniform Commercial Code, to facilitate wholesale asset theft by the protected class. U.S. Senator Elizabeth (Pocahontas) Warren is a longstanding member of the banking committee. This is what she has been doing. This is how she serves her donors. For decades, this woman has lied to the American people, and the Massachusetts voters always re-elect her, because her political campaigns are always well funded by the bankers whom she regulates. Anyone who is not a member of the oligarchy or protected class is a slave. Those who serve the oligarchs think they are above the slave chattel.

The modern American education system was designed by a gang of Marxist professors known as the Frankfurt School. They worked for the Institute for Social Research founded at Goethe University in

Frankfurt Germany in 1923. They were intellectuals, academics, and political dissidents who were dissatisfied with capitalism and fascism. They had the means and good sense to leave Germany when the NATS came to power. President Franklin D. Roosevelt (FDR) welcomed them with open arms and got them jobs at U.S. universities. FDR's maternal grandfather, Warren Delano Jr., made his fortune smuggling opium into China and the U.S., and this was the source of FDR's inherited wealth. Half of the Frankfurt gang went to Columbia University in New York, and half went to the University of California at Berkely. Within a short time, they infiltrated and took control of the university system and all the teacher colleges, and then the entire U.S. education system. The U.S. teacher colleges produce Marxist indoctrination specialists, not educators. Most U.S. teachers are Marxist to the core. All U.S. schools receive a monthly bulletin from the Southern Poverty Law Center (SPLC) which instructs teachers about important subjects like social justice, climate change and identity politics. The politicians send their kids to private schools, so they don't care about public education. What the politicians might not realize is that all the teachers come from the same place. Capturing the teacher colleges was a priority for the Frankfurt gang. There's very little donor money from educational book publishing, so the politicians don't care about it.

Trump appointed Betsy DeVos to be his Secretary of Education. Her husband is the founder of Amway, a pyramid network marketing scheme, and her brother Eric Prince founded Blackwater, the military contractor (mercenaries) who delete humans all over the world for money. Betsy accomplished nothing for U.S. education, which is the reason Trump appointed her—job well done. While U.S. kids are learning about pronouns and racism, Russian and Chinese kids are learning about science and math. U.S. schools are producing generations of lawyers and politically useful idiots, while Russian and Chinese schools are producing scientists and engineers. Education is a critical national security interest, and no one in the U.S. government seems to care about it, except the Marxists who run it. Evangelicals are mostly upset that boys are using the girls' restroom, and competing in girls' sports. As in the past, every future U.S. Secretary of Education will be a do-nothing stooge.

To be fair, the day Betsy assumed her role as Secretary of Education, she was confronted by a violent mob of Marxist protesters, and she was visibly shaken. She was never permitted to enter a school building. Trump's EPA Director, Scott Pruitt, resigned after receiving credible death threats to his family. Trump didn't have time to help Betsy or Scott because his re-election campaign began the day after he was inaugurated. Trump was too busy giving campaign speeches and promoting himself for the next four years. What will Trump do during his second term? Campaigning is the only thing he enjoys other than golf. Obama is the first U.S. president to have his primary residence built in Washington DC after leaving office. The U.S. has had an unelected ghost president for the last eight years.

The first priority of the American education system is preventing and defending against lawsuits from the American Civil Liberties Union (ACLU) and the Southern Poverty Law Center (SPLC). The second priority is maintaining a large staff of over-paid and useless administrators, fellow lodge brothers and sisters. The third priority is maintaining a big sports program budget, recruiting volunteers, and raising money. The fourth priority is Marxist indoctrination of American children. The last priority has something to do with educating children to prepare them for the workplace and political activism.

U.S. universities have been experiencing a revenue shortfall lately. China has stopped sending their kids to the U.S. These kids pay out-of-state tuition, and there used to be many thousands of them. Chinese universities are of better quality, much lower cost, and they don't have American-style Marxism. They prefer Chinese-style communism.

Virtue signaling is the public expression of sentiments intended to demonstrate one's good character or social conscience or the moral correctness of one's position on a particular issue. It is the act of saying one is good, without ever doing anything good. This pretend behavior is modeled and incentivized by the middle managers and oligarchs.

Identity politics is destroying America's morale. Our authoritarian rulers inform us, through their media monopoly, that we must accept as factual, whatever fictional identity is presented to us by grifters or people with a confused mind, or we risk being arrested for a hate crime. We must not offend a mentally confused liar by telling him he's a liar. That's a crime. White men should start identifying themselves as black female lesbians on job applications. This would improve their affirmative action status. They could still be white men on the weekends. A big downside is they might be forced to use the ladies' restroom at work. This would help the corporate executives meet their DEI goals and get bigger bonuses, and the white men would no longer be targets of racial and gender discrimination. We all need to be pretenders to get along in this Marxist insane asylum.

About 63 percent of the American population say their religion is Christian, and about 41 percent say they attend church once a week. The Super Bowl half-time show is a satanic ritual, and these Christians always clap like circus seals. America is a pretend society, where a lot of people pretend to be something they are not. Rachel Dolezal pretends to be black, but her biological parents are white. Elizabeth Warren pretends to be American Indian. Whoopi Goldberg pretends to be Jewish. Lia Thomas pretends to be a woman, but in high school she was a male. She still has her penis, and today she is a lesbian. RuPaul might be a man in the morning or a woman in the evening.

Jimmy Kimmel pretends to be a comedian. Propagandists pretend to be journalists. Rachal Maddow pretends to be honest. Lawyers pretend to be advocates of justice. Salesmen pretend to be your friend. Politicians pretend to care. Feminists pretend to be women. Drug companies pretend to help sick people. TV preachers pretend to be Christians. A lot of Americans pretend to be victims of some pretentious something, because victims are rewarded and they get attention. Mr. Trump also is not what he appears to be.

The transsexual movement is not a human rights issue. This is a wedge issue that Marxist political operatives use. The tranny movement is a profit boom for Big Pharma and the medical transition industry. The medical oligarchs are making a fortune selling the surgeries and life-long prescriptions the trannies need to pass as women. The tranny industry is a public-private partnership. They socialize the costs—American taxpayers and insurance customers pay for it. And they privatize the profits—Stryker Medical and the Pritzker family get rich. It's also a power play. The Marxists are demonstrating their power to impose their morals on a society that pretends to be Christian. When Americans go along with these pressure tactics, the Fascist oligarchs and their Marxist partners win. This is what is meant by a Fascist-Marxist hybrid government. The economic system is Fascism, because it is the most profitable for the oligarchs, who employ Marxist revolutionary political operatives to manipulate and control the slave population.

Americans are now required to use the term minor attracted person (MAP) in place of the word ped*phile. Human trafficking occurs in every country in the world, and the U.S. is the global capital of child sex trafficking in terms of both demand and supply. The normalization of sex with minors is a disturbing trend in the CW. The global elites hate children. They like to use them as sex objects and sacrificial offerings. Abusing children is a ritual that trains the elite mind to have no emotional attachment for humans. It's entertaining for them. And it produces valuable black mail.

For many years, Pakistani grooming gangs have operated in Great Britain with impunity and no possibility of prosecution. The British police are punished for racial discrimination if they attempt to arrest these animals. Britain also has a Syrian rape gang operating in Newcastle. Arresting them would be politically incorrect. For decades, celebrities, oligarchs, middle managers, and these middle eastern gangsters have abused children with impunity. Jeffrey Epstein, rumored to be an Israeli intelligence agent, ran a blackmail operation for decades in which he recruited underage prostitutes to have sex with politicians, oligarchs and celebrities, while being secretly video recorded. It's rumored that the Israeli government, the FBI, and others, have copies of these videos. It's also rumored members of Congress and a couple of U.S. presidents are actors in these videos. The identity of the persons featured in these videos is a national security secret (censorship). These elite MAPs are above the law. The FBI will continue to hide the identities of these elite MAPs to protect the blackmail operation. This is exactly how J. Edgar Hoover ran the FBI for five decades.

November 22, 2023 was the Sixtieth anniversary of the JFK murder, and CBS interviewed the Parkland Hospital doctors as shown in a YouTube video titled *"JFK's E.R. Doctors Share New Details About Assassination,"* CBS News November 2023. There were no new details. The five doctors are old men now, but still alive and well. They made exactly the same statements as they did sixty years ago. They said the wound on the front of the neck was an entrance wound, and the wound on the back of the head was an exit wound. Any deer hunter who saw the morgue photo knew that the frontal neck shot was an entry wound. The Secret Service would not allow the Parkland doctors to perform an autopsy, even after they explained that Texas state law requires this for gunshot deaths. The doctors said they could have the autopsy done in one hour. The Secret Service refused, and took JFKs body to the airport. The doctors were warned to stop talking about the frontal neck wound. The official autopsy at Bethesda Naval Hospital, said that the frontal neck wound was an exit wound and the wound on the back of the head was an entrance wound. On that day, the Secret Service violated Texas law, Parkland Hospital policy, and Secret Service protocols.

Colonel L. Fletcher Prouty wrote a book titled *The Secret Team: The CIA and Its Allies in Control of the United States and the World!* Col. Prouty was Chief of Special Operations for the Joint Chief of Staff during the JFK administration. He was portrayed as the character "Mr. X" in the Oliver Stone film *JFK*. He said he liked Donald Sutherland's portrayal of Mr. X. He was born in 1917 in Springfield, Massachusetts, and he became an Air Force Colonel. Col. Prouty was a decorated war hero who earned the trust and respect of everyone.

It was later said that Col. Prouty had some "association" with Scientology, but he was not accused of being a cult member. This looks like an attempt to smear his character. Perhaps L. Ron Hubbard tried to recruit him. Maybe Prouty was investigating Hubbard's mind control methods. At that time, it wasn't widely known that Hubbard was a serious fan boy of Aleister Crowley, and was deeply involved in black magic. Col. Prouty wasn't known to be a deceptive or dishonest person. That's how he was promoted into the positions he held. I believe every word Prouty says about dates, places, people, and what they did. Where I don't trust Col. Prouty's judgement is when he attributes motives to JFK's actions. I think he was biased and naïve in regards to JFK, who was a deceiver and a trickster. Most Americans are extremely naïve about the myth of JFK, who cultivated excellent propaganda. Many Americans believe he was America's greatest president (rubbish). Col.

Prouty doesn't hide the fact that he was a JFK fan boy. Someone who works in that job could be expected to be a president worshipper, and they were both from Massachusetts. Col. Prouty was a great American hero whose character was unassailable. He was never associated with trafficking drugs or humans.

Col. Prouty thought that the main reason JFK was deleted was because he made it known that the procedures for military procurement would be drastically changed during his administration. This would have gone unnoticed by the public, but it sent shock waves through the MIC community. They knew he would be re-elected, and then his brother would be elected, and so on. Something had to be done to stop this man, and his brother, who threatened their laundromat business. After the failed Bay of Pigs invasion in Cuba, JFK said that he would splinter the CIA into a thousand pieces and scatter it to the winds. He fired Allen Dulles, who was the first civilian Director of the CIA. Prouty said that in 1962 and 1963, Vietnam was not important. Not important to whom? Vietnam was of utmost importance to the Vatican, who claimed ownership of all arable land in Indochina. Vietnam was an extremely profitable slave colony that produced more than half the global supply of heroin.

Maybe Prouty wasn't Catholic. People who are not Catholic typically don't understand anything about this religion. People who are Catholic understand even less. Catholicism is a Babylonian occult mystery school religion invented by the Romans. JFK was a fourth-degree member of the Knights of Columbus, who regarded him as their most distinguished member. In the White House, JFK privately made statements that the U.S. would pull out of South Vietnam, and they would have to fight this war on their own, like the U.S. fought the Revolutionary War. He may have said those things at the White House, but he probably said something different to his pals at the Knights of

Columbus. Prouty said that he and General Krulak co-authored the National Security Action Memorandum (NSAM) 263 which described procedures to bring 1,000 troops home before Christmas 1963, and bring all troops home by 1965, but *no formal announcement would be made to the public*. This was a classic JFK misdirection maneuver. This was not an executive order, as claimed by the JFK apologists and pundits. No U.S. troops left Vietnam, and no such orders were given. JFK was the one who ordered the troops to go there in the first place. He escalated the war against Vietnam, and he fully supported that war until the day he was shot. Vietnam was Kennedy's war. In public speeches JFK was all about world peace and nuclear disarmament. At that time, most Democratic voters were not in favor of war. Privately, he knew he could count on war hawks like Robert McNamara to get the job done and save this slave colony for the Vatican. President Johnson later turned JFK's war into a successful business model. There were never any real war protesters. Young American men didn't want to be drafted, the female college students enjoyed the virtue signaling and drama, and the male protesters enjoyed the sex.

Col. Prouty observed several details about the assassination that were hidden (censorship) from the public. Most Americans are not aware that four bullets were fired at the president, and there was a minimum of two shooters. The two bullets shot from the front found their target. Agent Paul Landis found bullet number one in the back seat where JFK had been sitting. This bullet was in good condition because it went through soft neck tissue without hitting a bone, and it was stopped by the leather upholstery. Agent Landis said he placed the bullet on JFK's gurney, but the Warren Commission said it was found on Governor Connolly's gurney. The third "magic" bullet missed JFK and hit Governor Connolly in the front seat. The fourth bullet was fired at ground level from behind the president, and it went past the motorcade, hit a concrete curb, and then a fragment struck James Tague in the face. Prouty said that he was ordered to the South Pole to install a nuclear power plant, and the motorcade route was changed from the original planned route. The original route did not go through Dealey Plaza, where the limo slowed to six miles per hour and the ambush occurred. There were many violations of Secret Service protocol on that day. The president's car is supposed to travel at forty-five miles per hour, and it doesn't stop or slow down for any reason. In Dealey Plaza, there were no agents on building roof tops. All building windows must be closed while the president's car passes by, and Prouty explained how it's done. The Italian rifle and three shell casings found in the Book Depository Building had no fingerprints on the rifle or its internal parts. After Oswald was deleted at the police station, the rifle was taken to the morgue where his body lay, and then his right palmprint appeared on the rifle.

A journalist named Helmer Reenberg interviewed several eye witnesses who were present in Dealey Plaza. These video interviews can be seen at *www.youtube.com/HelmerReenberg*. None of these witnesses were called to testify at the Warren Commission. All of the eye witnesses said that, at the time of the shooting, they thought the rifle shots came from behind a wooden fence located between the Book Depository and the railroad. One witness said it sounded like two different rifles to him, but the federal agents reminded him that he was not an expert, and he agreed. All the witnesses near the grassy knoll saw a puff of smoke or a light flash behind the fence. After they read the newspaper articles, which described the official story and all the evidence found at the Book Depository, then they were convinced that all the shots must have come from the Book Depository. Some witnesses said they saw a man with a rifle at the open sixth-floor window. Most of the witnesses said they heard three shots, but some heard only two. The shots were all fired within six seconds. There was a sound recording of the shooting that came from a motorcycle policeman's radio. This was the same policeman who parked his bike, unholstered his pistol and ran up the grassy knoll to the wooden fence. The man standing behind the wooden fence ran away before the policeman could get to him. He left fresh footprints in the mud. The YouTube video titled *"Sound Designer Leo Chaloukian on his analysis of the JFK assassination tape"* by Foundation INTERVIEWS 2019, describes the recorded shots. In 1975, an FBI agent took this recording to a sound engineer and asked him to analyze it. He found there were four shots, and two of them happened at almost the same time. Prouty thinks Lee Harvey Oswald, Sirhan, and James Earl Ray were all fall guys.

It's interesting that the Warren Commission was controlled by LBJ, the man who had the greatest motive to remove JFK. Shortly after JFK's election, his brother Robert ordered J. Edgar Hoover to investigate the past crimes of LBJ, who was probably the most criminal president in U.S. history. Hoover was with a doubt the most corrupt law man in U.S. history, and he lived across the street from LBJ. Mac Wallace is believed to have deleted at least three people for LBJ, including his sister. His fingerprint was found on a box in the sniper's nest, on the sixth floor of the Book Depository. In 1963, there were only three television networks, and the Warren Commission was able to control the information viewed by the public. Because of the Internet, ordinary citizens can now access a lot of previously censored public information.

The fall guy is always a mentally unstable nutcase with no real motive. The media never told the public (censorship) that John Hinckley Sr. and George Bush Sr. were close friends. John Hinckley Jr. was declared not guilty by reason of insanity, and there was no trial for the Reagan shooting. Hinckley lived at St. Elizabeth's Hospital for several years, and he is a free man today. His psychotic disorder is in remission. Reagan was a changed man when he left the hospital. He seemed persuaded to change some of his political ideas.

JFK was a scoundrel. He had nice hair and gave good speeches, and he looked good on TV. He came across to the voters as presidential. American women were all in love with him. He was a genuine war hero. He commanded a patrol boat that was rammed by the Japanese. He was a good swimmer and rescued at least one sailor. The story was good enough, but then his father paid two of the sailors to give testimony to embellish the story, because the Kennedys wanted a biography to reinforce the coming political campaigns. His family's fortune came from smuggling whiskey during Prohibition. Joseph, his dad, was an aristocratic bootlegger. They got wealthy while other men went to prison.

President Eisenhower successfully made peace with the Soviets and tried to end the cold war. The *Atlantic* in their January/February 2013 Issue "*The Real Cuban Missile Crisis*" reported that, as soon as JFK became president, "he" ordered the military to stage Jupiter missiles with nuclear warheads in Turkey and Italy, aimed at the Soviets. The Soviets countered with missile bases in Cuba. In game theory, this was a tit-for-tat strategy, which the Russians almost always play. At the summit meeting, Kennedy was heavily medicated due to Addison's disease, which he hid (censorship) from the media. After the summit, it was announced that the Soviets would stop constructing their missile bases if Kennedy would remove the missiles he had deployed. The U.S. public were never told that the U.S. deployed their nuclear missiles first. This was a national security secret (censorship). Kennedy was a national hero because he made those bad Russians back down. This arrogant, reckless and dangerous man put at risk the lives of 30 to 40 million Americans.

In 2024 we have another drug addled Roman Catholic in the White

House who is working hard to provoke a nuclear conflict with Moscow. Ever since the Great Schism of 1054, the Vatican has wanted to delete Russia. For two hundred years, the Protestants warned about the danger of putting the Pope in the White House.

We live in a complicated world where some men cheat on their wives, but to embarrass the mother of his children the way he did is disappointing. He was very public with his extra-marital affairs, and the media celebrated his shameful behavior. This kind of immoral behavior can have serious consequences. He was a member of the liberal east coast aristocratic class. A more honorable man would have made an effort to be discreet. Maybe they had an open marriage. If Mrs. Kennedy was stepping out, she was very discreet about it.

JFK authorized the Bay of Pigs invasion, but he refused to authorize air cover. Without explanation his buddy McGeorge Bundy cancelled the planned air strike on three T-22 fighter jets that had been relocated to Santiago, Cuba. Air reconnaissance would have alerted the CIA that Castro had been tipped off and had a large force waiting for them to come ashore. Duplicitous behavior like this tends to anger goons with guns. E. Howard Hunt was furious that the operation he commanded had been compromised. This JFK story is important because a sitting U.S. president was gunned down by a federal agency that now controls the U.S. government and half the world.

Americans live in the wealthiest nation on earth because the middle managers have been told they can forever borrow endless amounts of fiat currency, and wash it around without any consequences to them. Americans live in the most powerful nation on earth, because U.S. military spending is greater than the nine next largest nations combined. America is the freest nation on earth, because trannies get their surgeries and medications paid by taxpayers and insurance companies—it's all free. Americans voted for this.

# White Problem

On May 13, 2023 U.S. President Joe Biden told graduating students at Howard University that white supremacy is "the most dangerous terrorist threat" to the American homeland. He has repeated this statement many times. This was not a gaffe. This was a policy statement. Van Jones, a popular cable news race agitator said, "We want the white people to go from being a majority to a minority, and like it."

"Demographics is destiny" is a basic policy statement of the Democratic National Committee (DNC). But anyone who dares to talk about Replacement Theory in relation to the migrant invasion is called a racist and a conspiracy theorist. After Donald Trump overwhelmingly won the 2024 RNC primary race in Iowa, the U.S. Marxist media moaned and groaned about how white, conservative Christian voters are a threat to American democracy. A popular new book being promoted by the legacy media is *White Rage: The Threat to American Democracy*, written by Tom Schaller and Paul Waldman. The authors of this book look like white men, but my guess is they don't consider themselves to be white men, because that would be self-hate. Their book summarizes the threat posed by this dangerous voting bloc. They say that white rural voters are racist, xenophobic, transphobic, homophobic, election deniers, vaccine deniers, and climate deniers. They own guns. They are guilty of slavery. They cause climate change. They believe in God and the Bible. They are conspiracy theorists. They are Christian nationalists. They are poorly educated. They deleted George Floyd. They are the worst people in the world. This book demonstrates the contempt that liberal, city-dwelling atheists have for the majority of Americans. Rural, white Americans are in fact angry about conditions, out of their control, brought about by Marxist revolutionaries who infiltrated and now control the U.S. government.

On March 5, 2024, the *Daily Mail.com* published the story "Biden Administration ADMITS flying 320,000 migrants secretly into the U.S. to reduce the number of crossings at the border." The migrant invasion is not a problem—it's a solution. White soldiers, white policemen, white fire fighters, white truck drivers and white farmers will all be replaced by more compliant and obedient migrants. Anyone who refuses the needle will be replaced with a less entitled person who has never heard of the Bill of Rights, and doesn't care. The migrant gets free stuff, and he will soon have a badge and a gun. Some sanctuary cities are already hiring migrants to fill the recruiting shortfalls in their police forces. The CW prioritizes the needs of migrants over the needs of tax-paying citizens.

The global population in 2024 is about 8 billion people. Asians are 59 percent, Blacks are 15 percent, and Whites are about 10 percent. The white population is declining rapidly due to low replacement rate. Van Jones thinks that 10 percent is a majority. He doesn't seem to be concerned that there are too many Asians in China, too many Blacks in Africa, or too many Arabs in the Middle East.

White men are not supposed to defend themselves when they are attacked by violent criminals. A Florida man named George Zimmerman was put through a national show trial because he shot a young black male, who spent the last four minutes of his life stalking and attacking Mr. Zimmerman. He jumped on Mr. Zimmerman, took him to the ground, pounded the back of his head against the sidewalk, and told him that he was going to delete him. The Marxist media and the mob insisted that Mr. Zimmerman is a white man, although his mother is Latina and his father is J*wish. He looks white enough, so the mob demanded he be charged with murder and found guilty. A liberal jury found him innocent. Mr. Zimmerman suffered a terrible ordeal. He changed his name and lives in hiding. All over America, prosecutors are charging white men for the crime of self-defense.

White men should not defend their property from violent criminals. They should run away. They can buy new stuff with their white privilege. Americans no longer believe in private property rights, not for white men.

A white cop from Minnesota named Derek Chauvin is in prison right now because a violent criminal, in his custody, died from a drug overdose. When Officer Chauvin arrested this man, he wasn't aware that the man had taken fentanyl. Officer Chauvin did his job, and used a restraining hold that he learned at the police academy. The autopsy, which showed no damage to the criminal's neck, was censored and not allowed in court, because the media had already convicted Mr. Chauvin, and the city managers were afraid of the mob who had already rioted and burned the city one time. A number of peer-reviewed studies have concluded that white police officers are not more likely to shoot minority suspects, but the Marxist mob and the media continue to repeat this narrative. One of these studies was conducted by a well-respected black professor of sociology at Harvard. He received death threats, had Marxist protesters in front of his house, and has lived in fear ever since.

In public schools, American children are taught about Critical Race Theory (CRT), which would be more appropriately offered as a graduate class in sociology. CRT training is also being required in workplaces across America. American children are told there is systemic racial bias wherever there are white people. White people must be made to suffer from white guilt, because they benefit from white privilege. People who never owned a slave are told they must pay reparations to people who have never seen a slave, outside of an Oprah Winfrey movie.

American corporations are fully engaged in the agenda to dispossess and discriminate against white men. Corporations must promote the climate change agenda, the queer agenda, and the agenda to discriminate against white males in hiring and promotion. In the U.S. it is still lawful to hire a white man, if he has high demand skills that are in low supply. He will get the challenging assignments and do the mundane traveling, but when a promotional opportunity arises, affirmative action policies must be rigidly adhered to. Exceptions are allowed if the white man is a member of an occult secret society or he was a nepotism hire.

Congress passed a law called the Opportunity Tax Credit. Corporations will be given a $10,000 tax credit per year for each illegal migrant they hire. It now costs 30 percent more to hire an American. Tyson Foods announced they will replace 40,000 American workers with migrants.

The worst mistake an American white man can make is to get married and have children. Fifty-six percent of all marriages end in divorce. When a white man gets divorced, a family court judge rules that he must surrender his home, his children, and half his assets, and he will pay alimony and child support for as long as the judge decides. Family courts incentivize women to get divorced. American women no longer need, want or like middle-class white men. If a woman makes an accusation against a white man, the courts must believe her, because women never lie, and the white man must be severely punished for doing something to a woman he has never seen. Donald Trump recently experienced this as a defendant in a New York civil trial. American women are in a perpetual state of being unhappy, dissatisfied, and disrespectful.

K.C. Johnson has written a book titled *The Campus Rape Frenzy: The Attack on Due Process at America's Universities*. Obama along with prominent democrat politicians have teamed with extremists and victim's rights groups to portray U.S. campuses as awash in a violent crime wave. If a female student accuses a white male student of inap-propriate sexual behavior, then he is guilty as charged. He will be immediately expelled from the university, and his records will indicate that he is a sex offender. After a college female drinks too much, and has consensual sex with a white man, her friends inform her that she is a victim of sexual crime, which must be reported to the authorities. The American "MeToo" movement states that anytime a female accuses a white man of inappropriate behavior, she must be believed without evidence, and the white man must be severely punished. For decades, everyone in Hollywood knew what Harvey Weinstein was doing with actresses. For about a hundred years, this was referred to as the casting couch. These adult women had consensual sex with him, because they wanted to join his club for money and fame. These Hollywood prostitutes knocked on his door, got on their knees and begged him for money and fame. Twenty years later, they joined the MeToo club to get press attention. They testified against him, and said he r*ped them. Contact with American women is high-risk and low-reward. One should try to avoid looking at them, speaking to them, touching them, or having anything at all to do with them. Most American women have mass psychosis-induced multiple personality disorders.

A white gen*cide campaign has been going on in South Africa for many years. Modern South Africa was founded by shipwrecked sailors employed by the Dutch East India Company. Dutch farmers were called Boers. When they arrived in South Africa, no one was living there. It was an inhospitable land full of swamps and insects. They made a treaty with the nearby Bantu people, and they co-existed peacefully most of the time, until the British arrived and did what they always do, steal everything. The Boers drained the swamps, farmed the land, discovered mineral deposits, and built an empire. The Boers did not displace a population group already living there, as with the American Indian genocide. There was no slavery. Black people moved into the area for low-wage jobs. Migrants came from India and many places. Blacks came from neighboring Zimbabwe by the millions. The country was a booming enterprise.

Then the Marxists came and did what they always do. An intense media campaign showed the world that the black people were a disenfranchised group being treated unfairly by the white people who had all the power and resources. To be fair, the Boers and the British were heavy-handed and greedy. The solution to this inequality was to disenfranchise the Whites, and transfer all power and resources into the hands of the afro-centric collectivists. South Africa is the only African nation with a significant white population. The white population of South Africa during the apartheid era was 20 percent, and now during the gen*cide era it is 7 percent. This is the kind of progress that Van Jones and his buddy Obama are working for in America. When white farmers are deleted, there is never a police investigation. Many members of the South African government, including President Cyril Ramaphosa, have repeatedly made public statements condemning white people. "White people's property should be expropriated. Whites should be treated the way N*zis treated J*ws." The U.S. and United Nations (UN) applaud the disappearance of white apartheid people in South Africa. Most CW states will not immigrate white refugees. Australia, New Zealand, the UK, Netherlands, and Russia are among the few nations who immigrate Boers. Russia needs farmers and English teachers, and many Boers have moved there. Land and homes in Russia are comparably inexpensive. White gen*cide is called a conspiracy theory by the Marxist media and their associates in the academic community. South Africa finally has democracy and freedom, now that the Marxists own and control the government. The white people who grow the food and generate the electricity are leaving as fast as they can. Unfortunately, many don't have the resources necessary to escape this Marxist dystopia. I've met a few white South African English teachers in Thailand.

Another persecuted white population group are the Amish and Mennonites, who are centered around Pennsylvania. The U.S. government has banned the sale of their food products and persecutes them relentlessly. They have groups living in several U.S. states. They should send a missionary group to Russia. Russians like Amish food, and Eastern Orthodox is compatible with Anabaptist. They would assimilate quickly. Some Canadian farmers are moving to Russia to escape the authoritarian government of Justin Trudeau and his self-imposed high cost of living in Canada. The CW rulers hate all Christians, especially the white ones.

The U.S. government is orchestrating an ethnic cleansing campaign against white men in Ukraine. Over the last two years, the population of Ukraine has decreased by 50 percent. More than a half million white men have been deleted in this war for profit. From the beginning of this war, U.S. officials and President Zelensky stated that Ukraine would fight to the last man, and this goal is being achieved. Ukrainian men are being kidnapped off the streets and sent into combat with little or no training. They are pushing these white men, to the last man, into a Russian sausage grinder. They are also conscripting women to the battle front. The Russians say they have many female POWs, and some were pregnant when they were captured. The smaller population group in Ukraine, who control the government and economy, made a political calculation that the larger population group must be eliminated, to the last man. Ukraine, or what's left of it, will soon be Europe's first J*wish state. One of Russia's primary goals is being achieved—a large number of Ukrainian NATS have been deleted. It appears that Zelensky and Putin share a common objective, to rid Ukraine of the Azov NATS battalions. These men are unruly and disobedient. Zelensky has removed all political opponents and opposition news outlets. His term as the elected president of Ukraine has expired. There will be no more elections in Ukraine. Zelensky is now a military dictator. The legal authority running Ukraine is the intelligence agency (SBU) which is heavily infiltrated by Russian spies. Zelensky has looted the Ukrainian Orthodox Church and jailed priests. Some analysts have commented that Zelensky is a Russian who recently learned to speak Ukrainian, and he still doesn't speak Ukrainian well, because it's not his native language. A political calculation has been made—white men must be sacrificed to the alter of the world revolutionary movement.

# Where to Go

Stay away from the CW countries which are under intense cultural Marxist pressure. The CW countries are coordinating a planned scarcity of resources. Crime and lawlessness are growing. Millions of security cameras have been installed. America is becoming a police state. Human rights are disappearing. Price inflation is intentionally being caused by the CW governments. A flu pandemic was engineered in one of their "military medicine" labs, and then weaponized against us. They will force every human to take the needle, on command, when they order it. Many African nations ignored the WHO mandates for lockdowns and needles, and they appear to have suffered much less injury compared to the CW states. The states who followed the WHO mandates suffered the most. The women in the CW states have been weaponized. Getting married and raising children in the U.S. is the worst idea a man can have. American society has made a political calculation that white men must be the new oppressed minority. The needs of migrants are prioritized over the needs of citizens. War profiteering is prioritized over all other considerations. The CW economies are collapsing under the weight of corruption and poor management. The CW nations are in a declining trend. Avoid conflict zones such as Ukraine, Isr*el, Myanmar, Haiti, Yemen, Ethiopia, and all of Africa. There are also countries where Americans are not welcome, such as Iran, Iraq, Cuba and North Korea.

That leaves about 90 countries to investigate. Several countries offer permanent residence or citizenship to people who can meet the requirements. Some countries offer citizenship by investment, but many of these are out of reach unless you are wealthy. In some countries you would need to remain in country, without leaving, for the period of time necessary to get permanent residence. In some countries you can get citizenship by marriage, or having a kid. There are a surprising number of states who offer citizenship by ancestry. The inability to get residency can make one feel insecure. If you have a problem, or make some mistake, the authorities can cancel your visa and force you to leave. You might be reluctant to invest or get married in a country where you can't get residency. There are nomads who bounce around different countries for years before they settle down—this is a lifestyle they enjoy.

The choice of where to live depends a lot on cultural preferences. There are several eastern European countries where people are mostly white, Christian, and conservative, such as Russia, Armenia, Albania, Hungary, Poland, Romania and Serbia. But Poland, Hungary and Romania are NATO member states. I would also avoid the Baltic states—these idiots are constantly goading Russia to attack them. NATO is a military alliance that exists for only one purpose, to provoke violence with Russia. A country that has nuclear missiles, has missiles targeted back at them. Nuclear war is survivable, but not if you are too close to the target.

Some men are attracted to Latin American culture. I think Latina women are drama queens. Residency is obtainable in a number of

South American countries, and the governments are peaceful and stable, for example in Uruguay and Paraguay. A lot of Americans enjoy living in Costa Rica, Nicaragua, Panama and Mexico. Costa Rica has become more expensive due to the inflow of so many Americans who drive up real estate prices. Columbia offers residency to those who buy land. These are terrific countries where an American can get residency. There are bad people in every country, but if you avoid them, they normally don't notice you. You should take precautions with your online activities no matter where you live. Andrew Henderson has a YouTube channel called *Nomad Capitalist*, and he recently posted a video titled *Fast Citizenship in Latin America.*

White Christian men might consider moving to Russia, where permanent residence is obtainable. Russia needs farmers and English teachers. They have labor shortages in many areas. Finding work or starting a business in Russia is not a problem. White people are not hated in Russia. Many Americans are living there for different reasons. If you have lived in the northern U.S. states, then the Russian winters won't be a problem. The outdoor winter activities you enjoy are there in abundance. There is no food scarcity in Russia. The government works hard to ensure an abundant supply of high-quality, affordable food. The grocery stores are full of everything. There are no bare shelves or waiting lines. Unlike the CW, the Russian government works to reduce inflation and improve living standards. The Soviet Union is long gone. Just fifty years ago, Russia was still a dark and scary place, but that history is over. There is no communism in the Russian government today. Marxism never existed in Russia. Marxism originated in Western Europe. The Russian people know what communism is, and most want no part of it. The Soviets were Bolsheviks, a different flavor of communism. Even now, the Russian people are not hostile to Americans. It's the U.S. government that aggressively pursues conflict and violence, and the Russians understand this. They know what the MIC is, and how it controls the U.S. government. The world revolutionary movement had its day in Russia, and most of those idiots are long gone.

The Russian government is family friendly, and they subsidize childbirth. They have too many old people, and they are trying to improve their demographics with new kids. There are many beautiful, feminine women in Russia. Russian women are not socially and mentally confused. They like to be women, and they like manly men. There is little racism in Russia. This is an immense country that spans eleven time zones. This civilization is more than 1,000 years old. They will be around long after the U.S. has destroyed itself. They have over 100 distinct ethnicities, with many languages and all the world's major religions are represented. In the western regions around Moscow and St. Petersburg, the majority of people are white Christians. They speak Russian, and support the Russian Orthodox Church. There are many autonomous regions, where certain ethnic groups are concentrated and have their own language and culture. The central government in Moscow provides infrastructure and public health support. These are the poorer regions, but everyone is a proud Russian. The crime rate in Russia is low compared to the U.S. There are no car jackings, race riots, or junkies living on the street. Russia has law and order. Things work there. The trains run on time. The streets are clean. There's no graffiti. There are few homeless people there because there is an abundance of government-provided housing. If there are homeless people, no one has seen them or seems to know where they are. There are many state-provided human services in Russia, which in the CW are controlled by profit-hungry oligarchs. Services such as electric power, gas for heating, internet, and cell phone are provided by state owned agencies, so the cost to the consumer is low, without all the profit taking middle men.

Russian citizens actually enjoy better rights than people in CW states. There are most definitely gay clubs in Moscow and St. Petersburg, but not in Chechnya or Dagestan. Homosexuality is allowed in Russia. What is not allowed is homosexual propaganda. There are no gay pride parades, or transexuals reading queer stories to children in libraries, or queers promoting queer stuff on TV or movies. Pakistani child sex grooming gangs don't exist in Russia.

Article 1 of the 1951 Convention of the United Nations High Commission for Refugees (UNHCR) defines a refugee as someone who owing to a well-founded fear of being persecuted for reasons of race, religion, nationality, membership of a particular social group or political opinion is outside the country of their nationality and is unable or, owing to such fear, is unwilling to avail himself of the protection of that country; or who, not having a nationality and being outside the country of his former habitual residence, is unable or, owing to such fear, is unwilling to return to it. Russia accepts political refugees, and Edward Snowden verified this fact. If you are outside the U.S., and you have not committed a crime, you can walk into a Russian embassy and ask to speak to an immigration officer.

The U.S. has the second largest number of prisoners worldwide, exceeded only by China, whose population is four times larger. In 2023, about 1.68 million people were incarcerated in the U.S., and roughly 1.69 million people were locked up in Chinese prisons. U.S. journalists and government whistleblowers are routinely locked up and deleted, and Julian Assange can verify this fact. Julian is an Australian journalist who will be extradited to a U.S. supermax prison where he will be deleted. He could have walked into a Russian embassy and saved himself, but he chose martyrdom. Anyone who speaks against the approved narratives of the U.S. media can be fired from their job or locked up.

Mr. Assange was indicted by the Trump administration, but it's likely Obama was managing the DOJ at that time. The U.S. has requested Julian be extradited to the U.S. for trial. Mr. Assange has been held in solitary confinement in London's Belmarsh Prison for the last five years. He has not been charged or convicted of a crime. His mental and physical health have deteriorated to the point that he is dying. President Trump's worst political instincts seem to be amplified with Mike Pompeo at his side. Pompeo and Hillary want Mr. Assange not alive. I would not be surprised to see John Bolton return to a second Trump administration. Trump has to do whatever Pompeo and Benjamin Netanyahu order him to do. Trump is weak and compromised.

A lot of Americans are living in China, because they like it there. I don't believe the U.S. government will start a war with China anytime soon, hopefully never. They will continue to work around the edges, publish propaganda, develop proxies and talk smack every day. For now, most of the bellicosity is about selling weapons to proxy states in the region: Australia, Japan, South Korea, Philippines, Thailand, and Taiwan. This is fearmongering to sell weapons. A lot of U.S. politicians have been taking money from the Communist Party of China (CPC), not just Joe Biden's son. There are beautiful Chinese spies sleeping with U.S. senators and congressmen. Most U.S. politicians admire the CPC and would like America to be more like them. If some idiot U.S. politician provokes a hot war with China, the U.S. embassy will evacuate the Americans ahead of time. Kevin Walmsley is an American living in Qingdao who operates a YouTube channel called *Inside China Business*. Kevin gives very insightful summaries of political, technological and economic developments in China, with no propaganda.

For certified American teachers, China can be a great destination. Right now, China has a shortage of native English speakers, and schools are paying good salaries to recruit new teachers. International schools and private schools in China have always paid good salaries. The same can be said about Vietnam, Japan, South Korea and Taiwan. A certified teacher in China can enjoy a good lifestyle and save for retirement. In Asia, teaching is an honorable profession, and teachers are treated with respect. Asian students and their parents are different from those in the U.S. These people are friendly and nice. Personal safety is not a concern for Asian teachers. There are no drugs, gangs, weapons, or career criminals in Asian schools. If you have a problem, talk to one of the Chinese teachers, and they will take care of it.

Many Americans are happy living in China, South Korea, Japan, the Philippines and other Southeast Asian countries. Andrew Henderson, who wrote *Nomad Capitalist*, recommends Kuala Lampur, Malaysia. Because I married a Thai woman, I live in Thailand more or less permanently. I live here on a visa that must be renewed annually, with quarterly online check-ins. In Thailand it is difficult to obtain residency, and impossible for most. Very few Westerners get permanent residency here. This is one of the main reasons I would not recommend settling in Thailand. Also, Thailand is practically a NATO member. I don't think most Thai people are aware that U.S. proxies in Thailand are arming and training the guerillas in Myanmar. The Thai government is well down the path of being used as a CIA proxy.

# PART II

## Thailand History and Culture

### How to Get There

Here's the bad news. You can't just show up here with nothing. That is guaranteed failure. It costs money to live here. Nothing is free. There are many videos on YouTube talking about how easy it is to live here for under $1,000 per month. That's wishful thinking. For one month, a tourist itemized his every little expense, and lived super cheap, so that he could make his video and prove how affordable life is here. He was in Chiangmai, and I think his budget did come in under $1,000. My living expenses are probably less than $1,000 per month, but I live in an agricultural district. I've never been to the entertainment zones, and I'm a boring old man. My cost of living is so low that I've never had a budget. In Bangkok or Chiangmai, you probably need more like $1,500 to $2,000 per month, especially for party people or men who like to rent bar girls. A lot depends on your habits and personal requirements. Without a doubt, there are Americans living a luxury lifestyle on $5,000 per month, which is the cost of an efficiency apartment, or a closet, in New York City. You need money for unforeseeable emergencies, and you need medical insurance, which is much more affordable for younger people. You need to keep enough money in a U.S. bank so that you can return to the U.S., or go to a different country and restart your life there. A rule-of-thumb I've heard is that you need one to two years of savings. Thailand has an excellent domestic brandy called Regency, but if you require French Courvoisier, then you need more income. I like coconut ice cream, but some foreigners require Haagen-Dazs. You can save a lot by buying domestic brands. Thailand gets much of their revenue from import tariffs, and less from income tax, which is how the U.S. operated for about 150 years.

You need to bring your finances with you. You likely won't find a job in any foreign country, unless it's teaching English. Some people come here as digital nomads. Online English teachers make more money than I ever did in a classroom, but I have more fun. There are many types of online jobs advertised on web boards. One nice thing about living in Thailand is that you can work fewer hours online and still get your bills paid and eat well. In the U.S., you might have to work two or three online jobs. Online job growth is an increasing trend, especially after the lockdowns. Companies usually pay hourly, and the work is mundane. I've seen jobs like medical records transcription, copy writing, and teaching English. Recently, there were a couple of young ladies here who were travel reporters for some magazine.

One young American man managed to save less than half a million dollars, which he invested in dividend stocks. He earns enough to live comfortably; he retired at age 35; and he does whatever he wants. A second young American man supports himself working as a day trader on the U.S. stock exchange.

A third young American man worked for the U.S. military in Afghanistan. He met a Thai girl online, and they talked at length. He came here, met her parents, and they got married. Like me, he has no desire to ever return to the U.S. While he was working as an English teacher, he learned how to make Shepard pies by watching YouTube videos. He started a business selling frozen pies to expats. His wife went back to school to get a masters' degree in English. He said that an international marriage can be challenging, but a patient man can make it work. They have two beautiful daughters and they are a happy family.

You can no longer have this lifestyle in the U.S., with the wife, kids and white picket fence. The authoritarians and their Marxist partners have destroyed all that. Some foreign men will buy an expensive home in Thailand, and title it in the children's names. They figure their children probably won't kick them out of the house they built. People like to feel secure in their old age. Most retirees here don't appear to be discouraged about the inability to secure citizenship. At our age, we won't have to deal with Thai immigration for long. The lifestyle we enjoy is worth the trade-offs, and we find work arounds.

How does one get a teaching job in Thailand? There are international schools where all classes are taught in English. There are private schools who like to hire native English speakers, because that's what the parents want. Normally, only large public high schools hire foreign teachers. Most of the schools outside of Bangkok and Chiangmai are public schools. There is a Catholic school in every large and medium-sized city. Most of the Muslim schools are located in the four southern provinces near Malaysia. There are private language businesses that offer English classes during evenings and weekends.

Liberal rich kids from the CW typically hire a travel agency that specializes in placing foreign teachers. For a fee, they will find you a job, process your documents, obtain your visa and work permit, and even find you an apartment near your school. They will help you get a bank account, and they will pay you your salary each month, with fees deducted, of course. If they find you an apartment, they will deduct a monthly fee for that. For anything they do for you, they deduct a monthly fee. Schools like to work with agents, because it's easy for them.

It's possible to find a job on your own. You don't have to hire an agent, but I'm sure it's faster and easier. There is a job board called *Ajarn.com* that lists available teaching jobs posted by the schools. A lot of hiring occurs without agents. Almost all the jobs posted are at schools located near Bangkok or Chiangmai, the two largest cities where there are more foreigners with children. Wealthier Thais enroll their kids in private schools. There will be an email address posted with a contact name. Send them an email saying you are interested in the position, and they will ask you to send pdf scans of your passport and university transcripts. If they think you are a good candidate, they will ask you for a phone interview, and it goes from there. For international calls I use a voice over internet service called Skype. There is a platform called Zoom, that is popular in America, and there is Microsoft Team Meeting. I don't know what communication platforms are used by Thai school recruiters. They have done this before, and they will tell you what they need from you. They will want a videoconference to evaluate your speaking ability and appearance.

I've done cold calling. I took my resume to schools near my home and asked to speak to the director or senior English teacher. It was fun. One public high school I visited was short-handed at that moment, and I started teaching there the next week.

At one private school, I met a beautiful young woman from Kenya who had been teaching there for some time. She spoke Thai and English fluently. She wasn't pleased to meet me. Kenya is a former British colony that has been pillaged by Freeloaders. I was surprised to learn how many teachers are here from Cameroon, South Africa, Kenya, and the Philippines, and some stay at these low-paying jobs for years. Maybe they have nowhere else to go. Some supplement their income by working part-time as private tutors. For years, I was under the false impression that all the foreign teachers are liberal white kids on extended vacation. Fifty years ago this was true. There are also a number of men from the entertainment districts who want to extend their stay in Thailand—they can't get enough ladyboy.

At a public high school, I met a young Thai teacher who surprised me because she sounded like someone from California. In fact, she sounded just like Jennifer Anniston, but she had never traveled to the U.S. I think some of the young ladies watch Hollywood films with subtitles. She was the second Thai woman I've met who has Jennifer Anniston's voice down pat. The sitcom *Friends* was subtitled and streamed to many countries.

The international schools in Bangkok and Chiangmai pay the highest salaries, and the classrooms are air conditioned. The pay is enough to live well and save for retirement. They only hire certified teachers with a Bachelor's in Education. If you are a certified teacher in the U.S., then you are qualified. If you are certified to teach other subjects like math or chemistry, then you will be paid more.

The private schools pay enough to live well, and that's about it—not much opportunity for savings. The classroom may or may not be air-conditioned. I think all the Catholic schools have air-conditioned class rooms. Many private schools hire non-native speakers if their accent isn't too strong, and they are paid less. To apply for these jobs, you must have a four-year college degree in any discipline, and you must have a Teaching English as a Foreign Language (TEFL) or a TESOL teaching certificate. For the TEFL certificate, you can go to a four-week school in Thailand that normally costs over $1,000, or you can obtain a

TESOL/TEFL certificate by taking a 120-hour online course that costs under $100.

The private language centers can hire foreigners who don't have a college degree, if they have good speaking skills and good appearance, and can show up sober. They are not required to hire teachers who are registered with the Ministry of Education, but they must furnish a work permit. These are the lowest paying jobs, and this is a for-profit business. These are weekend and after-hours classes for adults and children, and they focus on English conversation.

You might consider buying a secondhand car. You don't want a new car because of depreciation. I don't like riding a motorcycle in the rain. After five minutes I was soaked, and my shoes were full of water. It's difficult to keep electronics and paperwork dry. You might have an appointment where you need to show up on time and look presentable. You can't show up at school or a business meeting with your shoes full of water. The rain clouds can be unpredictable. They pop up and dump rain for several minutes. A motorcycle is the easiest vehicle to own and operate. For local driving, 125 horsepower is perfect, but for hill climbing at least 150 horsepower is required. To get to the waterfalls, we have to climb steep hills.

# Legal Advice from a Non-Attorney

If you are in Thailand, and find yourself in a difficult situation, i.e., you have pushed the boundaries of civilized behavior and done something extremely stupid, you need to contact a competent U.S. attorney. Benjamin Hart is the Managing Director of Integrity Legal, located in Bangkok. His firm specializes in helping Americans with immigration and other legal problems. They have a staff of Thai lawyers. His

YouTube platform, *Integrity Legal Thailand*, offers free legal advice and news updates. He can help with anything. He has lived in Thailand for sixteen years, and he earned Thai citizenship the hard way. Mr. Hart isn't the only US attorney here, but there aren't many.

If you are coming to Thailand, you need an international driving license, which is valid for six months. Your U.S. state driving license is not valid here. If you don't plan to rent a motorcycle or car, then you don't need an international driving license, and you can save $20. Unlike in the U.S., a person can go almost anywhere in Thailand using public transportation. The U.S. oligarchs are against public transportation because they want us to buy fuel, batteries, tires, paint, oil, and expensive maintenance, for the rest of our lives. For $50 a day you can hire a Thai taxi driver. I vacationed here many times without an international driving license. If you want to drive a motorcycle in Thailand, you need a motorcycle driving license, just like in the U.S. If you don't have a U.S. motorcycle driving license, I recommend you get one before coming here, and get it added to your international license. A motorcycle is convenient, less costly, and easy to park. You should wear a helmet. Thailand experiences a lot of horrific traffic accidents every hour of every day, especially with motorcycles. Getting a Thai driving license is easy. You just need to present a valid passport, a valid international driving license, and a health certificate from a hospital (no needle). The driving license tests in Thailand can be a challenge, mostly due to translation problems. I've done it and I don't recommend it. For the motorcycle license, I failed the written test three times. For the driving test, you must follow their instructions exactly. It is illegal to drink alcohol inside a motor vehicle, whether you are the driver or a passenger. In the U.S., this is called 'open container law.'

You need adequate medical insurance in Thailand. A traffic accident or a heart attack can get expensive. You are liable for any medical expenses on your behalf. Thailand has world class medical facilities and staff, and the costs are quite low compared to the U.S. There is a lot medical tourism in Thailand. People travel here to get joint replacements, sex change operations, all kinds of stuff. Thailand has government hospitals, private hospitals and private clinics. I recommend using all three. For small problems, I go to a local government hospital or a private clinic, and they charge foreigners the same price as Thai people. For an MRI, or surgery you will probably feel more comfortable at a private hospital. No one is going to pay your medical bills here. If you don't have adequate insurance, or you refuse to pay your bill, they have legal repercussions. They can take your passport. The Thai government doesn't budget for foreign freeloaders, and there is no support from the U.S. State Department. You need travel insurance, and then you need to find a medical policy. Medical insurance is the most expensive item on my expense profile, and it grows each year with age. I purchased my latest medical coverage from Bangkok Bank.

Recently, Thailand has been seeing more foreign tourists who behave badly. I think these people are stressed out from living in the CW. Some of them are just bad people. They get more stressed out by the horrible airline experience. By the time they get here, they are ready to explode with anger and frustration. A lot of Americans suffer from low impulse control and oppositional defiance disorder—life outside the U.S. is not safe for these people, and they should never get a passport. When your plane lands, you are mentally and physically exhausted. You should go directly to a hotel, sleep, and don't leave the room for at least twenty-four hours.

If a policeman directs you to pull over, do it. Follow his instructions and keep your mouth shut. He probably wants to give you a $20 traffic fine. Pay it, and be on your merry way. Americans are known for being drama queens, which can only make the situation worse. Recently, two men from New Zealand were pulled over, and they decided to fight with the Thai cop and take his pistol. In two minutes, they went from a $20 traffic fine to five years in prison. I like the movie *A Prayer Before Dawn*, starring Joe Cole. It's a true story about a white man who made bad decisions and was sentenced to two years. This film gives an accurate portrayal of life inside a Thai prison.

A lot of Americans seem to think U.S. law follows them across international boundaries. This is not true. A U.S. citizen needs to obey the laws of the host country that has granted visa entry. The Thai government tries to follow international norms, but there are some differences between Thai law and U.S. law. Shoplifting is legal in the large U.S. sanctuary cities, but it is not legal here. Blacks are privileged citizens in the U.S., but Thailand never had African slaves. No one owes anyone reparations here. The Thai Royal Family and the Thai oligarchs are the only privileged minorities here. Whatever your skin color might be, you should not steal things here. I recall some American professional basketball players who were arrested at a shopping mall in China. They were surprised to learn that shop lifting is a serious crime in China. The U.S. State Department intervened for these black celebrities, but the State Department won't lift a finger to help you.

You do not want to get into a violent altercation here. Violent behavior is tolerated and encouraged in the U.S., but not here. Some Americans drink too much alcohol and forget where they are. I drink at home. I don't drink in public. I get sleepy and stupid, but a lot of people want to fight. If you cause physical injury to a Thai citizen, this could result in prison time, the first time. If you do something stupid, apologize and try to settle things. If someone else does something stupid, apologize and walk away, if you can. In the unlikely event that you find yourself in a self-defense situation, get out of there as fast as you can, get to the nearest airport and buy a ticket on the first flight out. Your image has likely been captured by a security camera or a cellphone. Thai cops are good with computers. You do not want to talk to them if you can avoid it.

Some Thai men are smaller than a lot of Europeans or Americans. He might be 5'6" tall and weigh 140 pounds, but don't deceive yourself. There is nothing about his appearance that might warn you he once worked as a prize fighter. A few men here have trained in Thai boxing. You might be a tough guy, but these guys are tougher, and they outnumber you. Most Thai men have never fought in the arena, but if you cross paths with a boxer or an ex-military guy, you are going to have a bad day. Apologize and walk away. Here's a hint about the identity of the man who will send you to the emergency room or the morgue. He's the quiet man sitting behind the drunk man doing all the talking. It's unlikely you will ever have a problem with a Thai man. Foreigners are the greatest threat to your freedom and well-being.

If you enter Thailand with cannabis oil or vaping devices, you could be arrested. A powerful Thai family owns the tobacco monopoly, and they don't approve of vaping or imported contraband. If you need to do this, don't come here. I see Thai guys vaping, but not in public, and they are Thai citizens.

Methamphetamine is the drug of choice in Asia. Some men think it makes them more productive and competitive. (That's what Zelensky says about cocaine.) The Thai word for meth is *YaBa*, medicine crazy, so they understand what it does to a person. Most of the meth is trafficked from labs in Myanmar. Few Thai men smoke cannabis. Opium can only be found in the hilly border regions near Myanmar, and Thai people don't touch it. The illicit drug market works the same in Thailand as it does in the U.S. All the drug dealers are confidential informants. If you visit the border areas and want to sample some products, don't bring anything back. You don't want to go through a check point with that stuff. The drug laws here are harsh. Many years ago, European hippies would go live in the border areas where they could find opium. They would become addicted and they wouldn't leave. Some of these guys over stayed their visa by years before they were caught.

The Thai government monitors social media platforms. If you post insulting photos, insult the royal family, or insult a Thai business, the police will know about it almost immediately. Several years ago, two American homosexuals posted a photo on Facebook showing one of them with his pants pulled down at a landmark Buddhist temple. They were detained at the airport; their flight left without them; and they got off with a small fine.

To have sex with under-age minors, the best place to do that is in the U.S. or Britain. Don't come here. Thailand is not an MAP-friendly environment. Human traffickers in the U.S. have all kinds of kids for rent. Children are bought and sold daily at the U.S. southern border. This is what freedom means in the U.S. Crimes against children are not tolerated in Thailand.

If you plan to be outside the U.S. for more than one year, it's probably a good idea to get a durable power-of-attorney (POA). Soldiers often do this before they deploy to combat. You might need someone to wire transfer money from your bank account. Selling something like a house, automobile or a boat requires a notary stamp. To get a notary stamp, you must see an American lawyer or make an appointment online at a U.S. consulate. Most Americans don't have anyone in the U.S. they can trust. I am fortunate to still have two living uncles, and they have helped me with some problems I didn't foresee. It's a lot cheaper and easier to get a POA from inside the U.S..

Visa requirements are no joke. Thai Immigration follows the letter of the law without exception. You might be an important person where you are from, but here you are just another visa holder. They have computer databases, and they know where you are. If you overstay your visa by one day, they will know it and come looking for you. The expiration date of your passport is six months before the date printed on your passport. If your passport will expire within six months, you can buy a ticket, but the airline won't let you board. You are required by law to carry a copy of your passport anywhere you go. Take photos of all important documents and save them somewhere. Non-immigrant visas must be applied for at a Thai consulate outside of Thailand. You can't come here on a tourist visa and then apply for a non-immigrant visa in-country, not without legal help.

To do any type of work in Thailand, you must have a work permit issued by the Ministry of Labor. Thailand has protective labor laws designed to shield Thais from foreign labor. There is a list of jobs or professions that only Thai people may do. You cannot work as a tour guide, street vendor, trucker, or repairman. Working without a permit can result in immediate deportation. Volunteer work requires a volunteer visa. Work without pay requires a work permit. If you want to work as an independent journalist, you must have a media visa. The U.S. doesn't protect citizens from foreign labor competition, so there are no restrictions on what a foreigner may do in the U.S., but I think the U.S. still has something called a green card. There are a limited number of jobs that an American can do in Thailand: English teacher, real estate agent for foreign buyers, insurance agent for foreigners, bar owner, guest liaison at a large hotel, foreign chef at a large hotel, and online work. A foreigner can be employed by an agency that sells to foreign clients, but the foreigner cannot own the agency without a 51 percent Thai partner. Certain technical specialists are in short supply.

I met a young American man from Michigan who works in Bangkok as a certified gemstone appraiser. You need a work permit to do any of these jobs. To operate a business in Thailand, the business must have majority Thai ownership—most expats have their business in their wife's name. Establishing a business with people you don't know is always a bad idea. If you want to own a bar, then you need to own it outright. This is one business where you don't want a partner unless she's your wife. The retirement visa is easy to get, but you cannot get a work permit with this visa because you told Thai Immigration that you are retired. You can get a work permit with a marriage visa. English teachers and business owners normally have a B visa. There are many categories of visas to choose from. If you are already here on a non-immigrant visa, you may change to a different non-immigrant category without leaving the country. I changed from a retirement visa (easy to get) to a marriage visa (less easy), because I wanted to be a school teacher, and I wasn't required to leave the country or hire an attorney. Thai immigration lawyers know how to acquire all the different visas, but it's normally a straight forward process, and no attorney is required. The folks who work at Thai Immigration can speak English.

My wife owns a registered pistol, and the Thai police have never asked her about it. I like for her to have a firearm when I'm travelling and she is home alone. When she bought it, I had been living in the U.S. and still had the paranoia that comes from living in a danger-ous and violent society. Home invasions are uncommon in Thailand. Foreign ownership of firearms is no longer permitted, and I think it's a bad idea anyway. I don't need a gun, but I sometimes wish I had a .410 shotgun for these big rat snakes. Some people like sport shooting as a hobby, and there is a gun range not far away. I see a lot of Thai guys shooting air pistols, and they have competitions. An air rifle, cross-bow, spear, knife, and sword are all approved toys for the foreigner, and no registration is required. To legally transport a firearm in Thailand, it must be in the car trunk, unloaded, with registration papers. In the unlikely event that a policeman would look inside your car trunk, you need a story about why you are transporting a firearm. You are either going to or coming from a practice range, and you need to tell him where it is located. He has the right to ask these questions, and you have an obligation to answer. Gun ownership is not a problem in Thailand—you just have to follow their rules. Only policemen and soldiers are licensed to carry.

Sending and receiving mail can be challenging for expats. I have not found one U.S. company or institution that will send mail to an address outside the U.S. For several years, I have maintained a mail delivery service with United Parcel Service (UPS). My only U.S. address is a UPS store. They collect my mail and deliver it to me when I request it about once or twice a year. The annual cost of the service is around $150, and I pay shipping when they send me mail. I ask them to send my package via first class U.S. mail because that's the lowest cost option. It normally takes two to four weeks to arrive. UPS and the U.S. Postal Service (USPS) don't seem to have a friendly relationship. They are competitors even though the USPS can't compete because they don't offer as many services, and their mail service and customer service is not so good. UPS and DHL will not deliver to a USPS post office box. I sent my tax return via DHL to a PO Box because that was the only address given in the instructions, and it was returned to me. In Thailand, I have two options for sending mail. It costs about $11 to send a letter via USPS, and it usually takes a month or more to get delivered. USPS only offers tracking to U.S. Customs in New York, and the letter normally sits in Customs for about a month before it gets sent out for delivery. For $45 I can get my letter delivered in about one week, and I get tracking all the way to the delivery address. At the Thai Post office, I have to ask for Courier Express service. The Thai postal service has a contract with DHL, which Thai postal employees have never heard of, so don't ask for DHL. I'm not going to ask my uncles to use their home address, or to manage my mail for me.

For calls to the U.S., I use a voice over internet application called SKYPE. It normally works well enough. I can make calls to the U.S., but no one can call me. When I place a call to someone, they see an odd-looking random number on their caller ID, and most people won't answer my call because they think it's a scammer or a robocall. For about $75 per year, SKYPE can give me a U.S. phone number to show up on caller ID, but I haven't done that. Verizon offers an international phone number for about $200 per month, but I don't make many calls, and I don't like to deal with U.S. cellular companies, who all seem to have horrible customer service.

U.S. banks and brokerage firms are hostile toward expats. I think this is a recent development. I don't recall all this hostility towards expats in the past. I get a lot of passive aggression from female customer service agents. The mailing address I use on my bank account and brokerage account must not contain the word BOX. When the computer algorithm sees the word BOX, it automatically flags my account, and then I have to talk to one of these awful female customer service agents. I always use the word APT or SUITE in my mailing address. If you don't have a physical street address where you sleep at night, the banks and the brokerage firms will close your accounts, and you can't have a credit or debit card either. These are mean people. I never say that I live in Thailand. I'm either on a temporary work assignment or a long-term vacation. The truth is that I am not a legal resident of Thailand because I am here on a non-immigrant visa, and my passport is proof of this fact. I pay county, state and federal taxes every year to the U.S. If the bank closes my account, then I have no way of paying my taxes or receiving a pension. Social Security will direct deposit to any foreign bank that has a SWIFT code. I'll bet it took a class action lawsuit to get that done. China has SWIFT at the moment, but they probably won't have it for much longer. Russia was sanctioned out of SWIFT banking. My Thai bank account must be reported annually to the IRS on Form 8938 Foreign Account Tax Compliance Act (FATCA). If my account balance exceeds $10,000, then I must also file a Foreign Bank Account Report (FBAR). These are some of the inconveniences of living abroad.

You do not want to be deported from this country. They don't just give you a ride to the airport. The deportation process is a punishment all its own. You will be taken to an immigration detention facility for out-processing, which can take thirty days or longer. This place is worse than prison. There are men there from fifty countries. When you arrive, you are placed in a que. All the men who came before you will be processed out before you. You will definitely lose weight and hope you don't get ill. No one is going to help you.

# A Tale of Two Cultures

Millions of Americans are afflicted with a personality disorder called arrested development. Their physical body grows and ages normally, but their mind never gets past the maturity level of a fifteen-year-old. This mental disorder is endemic to America. Thankfully, we don't see this much in Asia. It's refreshing to go to another country and meet young people who are mature adults. We have two teenage Thai nephews who are more mature than most American adults. This disorder is characterized by a lack of responsibility, a lack of discipline, laziness, selfishness, narcissism, a lack of empathy, and willful ignorance about anything not related to social media and entertainment. They believe that life is supposed to be a party. Work is something other people do. Actions don't have consequences. It is the responsibility of government, or someone else, to pay the bills. Freedom means decadence. Entertainment is the only reason for existence. The boys watch sports and play video games all day. The girls do text messaging and play games on TikTok and social media. Sympathies to anyone unfortunate enough to become the spouse or child of one of these worthless idiots. I have read that the oligarchs don't allow their children to spend more than two hours per day on social media because they know about the addictive and harmful psychological effects of the social media platforms they foist on the public.

Ruminating is another personality disorder endemic to the CW. Americans, especially young people, constantly obsess about their perceived victimhood. Climate change is destroying the planet, and killing millions of people, and because of this, I don't have a future, and someone is at fault, and something must be done. I've thought about this a lot, and my friends and I have watched all the media propaganda, and we talk about it endlessly. It's time for action. Let's go sit on the freeway, block traffic, create a safety hazard, and act like morons. These people obviously don't work or have any responsibilities. "How dare you!" says Greta Thunberg, a high school dropout. She is an actress playing a part. Both of her parents are actors. They don't care about climate change. What they care about is money and fame. When she's doing her media stunts, she always has this evil little grin and self-satisfied expression as if she is thinking, *Look at all these fools following me around and listening to my every word.* There are now millions of teenage girls who mimic Greta's odd behavior. They even mimic her Asperger's syndrome. Americans ruminate about everything. They are constantly searching to find new ways to be victims, because victims get attention. They make themselves and anyone around them miserable.

The children and grandchildren of German and Ukrainian NATS

ruminate about their hatred. From birth, all they ever think about is deleting Russians. It's Russia this, and Russia that, all the time. The dictator Putin must go. What a pathetic life. Russian scholars agree that Stalin was a successful psychopath. He is the one who starved and deleted all those ethnic Ukrainians in the 1930s. Stalin persecuted all Russians everywhere. He died in 1953. The Soviet Union was replaced by the Russian Federation in 1991. There is no Stalin. There is no communist Soviet state. This generational revenge thinking is irrational, and it never ends. Now Russia has this hostile, U.S.-installed next-door neighbor that ruminates, fires artillery at civilians 24/7, and organizes ter*rist attacks inside Russia.

I feel some sympathy for many black Americans because they seem to ruminate all the time about perceived microaggressions and racism. The race hustlers and poverty pimps constantly reinforce their victimhood to get public funding, and motivate them to be failures, to get more public funding. They can't accomplish anything in life because of imaginary racism, so they don't try. They need racism to justify laziness, apathy, and the victim mentality. Successful black people don't waste time ruminating. They know American history, but they don't dwell on it. They re-build Black Wallstreet. They try to keep a positive attitude and move forward in life. They don't blame others for their mistakes or misfortunes. Many Blacks seem to have a religious outlook that keeps their mind positive and focused on self-improvement and success. A big thank you to the millions of American Blacks who refused the flu needle. They reminded us about the Tuskegee Syphilis Study conducted between 1932 and 1972 by the U.S. Public Health Service and the Centers for Disease Control (CDC). Black Americans understand vampire culture, and they don't like needle pushers. They understand civil disobedience. Robert F. Kennedy Jr. has written an interesting book about the coughing flu,

*The Wuhan Cover-Up and the Terrifying Bioweapons Arms Race.*

The trouble with most white men is that we believe certain propaganda myths, and we are not going to give them up. Our minds are clouded by irrational thinking because of these myths. This magic, colored glass in front of our eyes hypnotizes us, and makes us stupid. Intelligent and clever people gave us these myths, which were carefully crafted and handed down through the generations. Our history textbooks were written by Marxist propagandists, like Howard Zinn, a professor at Columbia University. We believe things that are not true. We have been hood-winked and bewitched.

White American men also have it rough. A lot of middle-class, white men lost their jobs because they refused the flu needle. The GOAT tennis player from Serbia was shut out of his sport in the CW because he refused the needle. He seems like a nice man, and he's very intelligent. He was raised in a part of Europe where people understand NATS. He appears to be on someone's enemy list, and he persists with his refusal to obey the N*ZI needle pushers. He is a disobedient white man who does not comply with government mandates. He is a threat to national security. Even sports celebrities are becoming victims of these occult vampires. A lot of white Americans grew up poor. We got beat up at school. We can't get anywhere in life unless we pass tests and more tests because we are never good enough. American prisons have a lot of white men in them. White men get deleted in wars; they get shot up; they lose body parts, and they lose their minds. Most white women are no good, so a lot of us are lonely bachelors. If we make the mistake of getting married, divorce is inevitable, and then we lose everything we worked for and care about. We have to listen to this nonsense about white privilege all the time. We are accused of racism when we haven't done anything to anybody. We are under constant attack by the revolutionary legal system and the Marxist media. I ruminate.

Thai people don't ruminate much. They don't have time for it. They have responsibilities and work to do. They more or less live in the moment. Life has its challenges, but they always find a way to enjoy life. Their families are their purpose in life. They don't seem to get stressed out about fashionable ideas. Vietnamese people are amazing. They suffered slavery for over one hundred years at the hands of the French, and then 3 million of them were deleted by the Americans. Since their liberation in 1975, they have created an advanced, remarkable civilization. The older generation still carries a grudge, but they don't sit around and ruminate and feel sorry for themselves. The CW made that beautiful country a hellish nightmare for those beautiful people, and yet, here they are. Asians tend to be resilient—they are the 59 percent club. They are a kind and moral people. The Vatican are morally depraved degenerates. The Vietnamese have taught the world an important lesson: It is possible to survive these occult monsters and live to see a better day. Let's hope the Africans will see this lesson, as they cast off their French vampires, with a little help from Russia and China.

Virtue signaling is another hallmark of modern American society. This is the art of telling everyone what a good person you are, without actually doing anything good. Social media is driving this insane behavior. Americans have always done it, but social media can potentially connect to a large audience. It multiplies and amplifies this disgusting behavior. It's another mind virus. This is self-aggrandizement and self-gratification. It's sadly ridiculous. These people are mentally ill.

Woke culture is closely related to virtue signaling. The two personality disorders are normally present at the same time. Wokeness is the belief that all minorities and women are long oppressed by a white male patriarchy, and this situation needs to be rectified, and there must be retribution against evil white men. One way to rectify this situation is for white people to publicly demonstrate white guilt at every opportunity. American Whites are collectively guilty, so we must publicly and continuously atone for our microaggressions and express remorse for the behavior of our ancestors. The white male evil doers must be punished. White women are now too virtuous to be seen in public with an evil white man. White women are even changing their racial identities so they can be included in an oppressed minority and join the victim club. This makes them feel more virtuous. Rachael Dolezal became black and Elizabeth Warren became an American Indian. The woke mind views Islamist extremists as oppressed minorities. A dedicated woke activist will participate in political protests demanding fairer treatment for terr*rists who throw queers off buildings and cut off the heads of Christians and journalists with a serrated knife. Christians are another target of woke activists. During the Crusades, the evil white Christians invaded M*slim lands, which included Pal*stine. From woke history we know that violence was never directed in the opposite direction. Woke history informs us that M* slims never invaded European states because Islam is a religion of peace. Professor Bill Warner has posted an excellent sixty-minute documentary on YouTube titled *"Why We Are Afraid,"* which showcases his historical research on political Islam.

One's role models influence one's behavior. The most influential role models for CW women are entertainment celebrities, all of whom belong to bizarre religious cults. These are the world's most narcissistic and vapid pretenders. The female role models in politics and media are rude, opinionated, and obnoxious. Feminist role models are aggressive and combative. TikTok influencers suffer from multiple personality disorders and insanity. The big and beautiful crowd convinces women that being fat is good and healthy. The food industry promotes this obesity culture to sell more processed food, and these fat women keep shoveling that poison into their pie holes. Oprah promotes New Age religions non-stop—she promotes anything that's not Christian. The boss bitch role models are insufferable, mean and calculating predators. Many decades ago, a common job interview question was, "Who are your role models, and why?" The answers can be revealing. Today's human resources professionals, who are almost all woke liberal females, want to know about our pronouns.

American men also have poor role models. The Tate brothers are a sad reflection of modern male culture. They promote a culture of materialism, hyper masculinity, vanity, misogyny and narcissism. They operate a social media webcam platform where men pay money to watch women get naked and perform fetish rituals in front of a camera, and solicit donations. It's an entertainment platform. It provides an income to women who have no marketable skills, and have only one sellable asset. The Tate brothers should be nominated for a Nobel Peace Prize, because they have developed a new and improved business model for pimping. Their employees are not exposed to the risk factors that prostitutes normally encounter on a daily basis. They have made the world a safer space for working women. They also sell educational programs to teach men how to be jackasses, like them. After decades of exposure to armies of male celebrities who are effeminate, homosexual, transexual, metrosexual, narcissistic, beta clowns, men are craving a more masculine role model that doesn't bend to the whims of selfish and manipulative women. The Tate brothers manipulate women to perform self-degrading and outrageous behavior for money. American men find the Tate brothers to be empowering, refreshing, and uplifting. It seems to somehow grow their self-esteem, which has been hammered into the dirt by the media. The Tate brothers profit from social dysfunction. I have nothing against them. They are living life on their terms. Their business model is legal. I don't see crime victims. I wish them happiness and long life. I just think they have an oversized influence on young men. They are naughty boys and poor role models. They are being severely punished by the Romanian and British governments for crimes that don't yet exist, like refusing to wear a dress.

The American comedian Katt Williams has demonstrated that men in the entertainment industry who wear dresses are catapulted to fame, while men who refuse to wear dresses are pushed aside. The Tate brothers are getting the Trump treatment. A public example must be made of these two ideologically non-compliant white men, who are actually black. Their father was a black man, who was a CIA agent stationed in London. Their mother was white, so that's white enough for a high-tech public lynching. It seems like there are no civil rights in these two countries.

Britain and Romania are persecuting these two entertainment-industry black men, because they operate under the "international rules-based order." They don't have civil law in these two countries—they have CIA law. The entertainment industry seems obsessed about encouraging black male entertainers to wear dresses. These two black men who ride around in private jets and luxury sports cars, have become proud and uppity, and they have to be brought down. These two NATO states should be avoided by travelers. Britain, where the Tate brothers grew up, has always been a police state run by occult gangsters. There are few good things about Britain: shepherd's pie, fish and chips, football clubs, rock music, Doc Martin, and Mr. Bean. I'm guessing the Tate brothers are living in Romania for business reasons. It looks like someone in Dubai has given them assurances about living there, and Andrew recently converted to Islam, so it appears they can resume their entertainment business in the United Arab Emirates. They will become little fish in a big pond, but they won't be arrested for refusal to wear a dress.

Sports celebrities are the world's most entitled, narcissistic, and spoiled brats. Many of them are violent criminals. American men are mesmerized by the money, fame and gold diggers that surround their sports heroes.

Hollywood glorifies violent tough guys like cowboys, cops, pirates, mercenaries, drug pushers, and gangsters. There is a group of niche actors who are military recruiters for the U.S. Department of Defense (DOD). They are the heroes in war films. After two hours of watching Sylvester Stallone, Matt Damon or Tom Cruise, teenage boys want to be fighter pilots, spies, knuckle draggers, snipers, and special ops goons. Little American white boys can't wait to grow up so they can be heroes and delete all those brown sub-humans who are invading America from 10,000 miles away. We've got to fight them over there so we don't have to fight them here. DOD and Hollywood have had a long and profitable partnership from the beginning of Hollywood history. They are the primary propagandists, salesmen and military recruiters for the MIC. Hollywood also influences men in another direction. The goal is to produce confused minds that can be forged into an army of Marxist political activists and useful idiots. This is not about entertainment—this is war propaganda. Most CW male role models are queers and Marxist activists. They are culture warriors who wear dresses.

American trannies are the world's most obnoxious and aggressive political activists. They constantly harass white men with their personality disorders and arsenal of pronouns. They try to get white men fired from their jobs and locked up for hate crimes. This wedge issue weeds out ideologically non-compliant white men. It empowers emotionally dogmatic authoritarians to attack the non-obedient. Real men will never submit to this queer, authoritarian bullying. It seems like every member of ANTIFA is a tranny or a dyke, and they all seem to come from privileged backgrounds. This is how wealthy, white, woke mothers contribute to the revolutionary movement. Raising a violent, queer political activist gives meaning to the lives of these depraved, liberal, rich women, and makes them feel more virtuous for sacrificing a child to the world revolutionary movement. They sacrifice their children to the alter of woke virtue. Insane behavior has been weaponized against Americans. We are all victims of the Marxist culture war.

American men have few positive role models. Joe Rogan is the most popular podcaster in the world right now. He was always a leftist liberal. He lived in liberal cities his whole life. He thinks Austin, Texas is a conservative city. He seems to be experiencing a genuine, gradual transformation as he educates himself and his audience. He is waking up, and he is waking up a generation of propagandized men. He will never be a right-wing conservative, but his views have definitely moderated over the years. He has put in the work and become highly successful. I admire him because he motivates men to learn new things and try to understand the complicated manosphere we live in. Men need food for their brains. Mr. Rogan has a reputation for treating people fairly. How people live their private lives is their business, but I wish he would stop drinking and smoking during his shows. Young people who are watching look to him as a role model. He might not view himself as role model, but he could be a better role model without the substance abuse on video.

One brave and honest man I have always admired, who has been consistent with his principles and advocacy for Americans, is Senator Rand Paul. His father, Ron Paul, was a great American congressman. Thomas Massey is another great American leader of the same caliber. They must be friends, because they both live in Kentucky, and probably see each other in the halls of Congress. These men don't work for the MIC or the Zionists. They work for the people who voted for them, and the same is true of Marjorie Taylor Greene. It's fine if you don't like her personality, but she works for the voters in her district, not the MIC and the Federal Reserve Bank. She often gets death threats, and she's been swatted by the FBI at her home. Americans have very few representatives in government. Out of 535 Congress members, White American Christians have at most three representatives—the rest represent self-interest, Zionism, the MIC, and the Federal Reserve. At every level, the U.S. government is a laundromat. American voters didn't like Ron Paul in 2008, and today they don't like his son Rand because these two politicians are generally opposed to foreign wars. American voters want politicians who will protect and grow their good-paying jobs at the war factories. Americans feel reassured when the U.S. military is stomping on people who are different. Americans like imperial power. Other nations must bend to our will. We are G*d's chosen people because we support Zionism. Ron Paul projects weakness because he doesn't prioritize aggression, and he thinks people with different cultures and skin tones still have human rights. Ron Paul and his son are un-American.

Thai people are not pretentious. What they think they are, and what they say they are, is what they are. They live in reality. Thai female celebrities tend to be soft spoken, polite, feminine, pretty, and not fat. Thai male role models tend to be masculine, soft spoken, polite, handsome, and not fat. Thais work harmoniously well in groups. Whatever the job is, they jump in, and everyone seems to know what to do, and they seem to enjoy working together. It seems every young lady in Thailand is obsessed with K-pop singers. These are effeminate Korean boy bands. Their favorite boy band is a group called BTS. Korea has a large entertainment industry that produces endless Netflix videos. Absent from Korean movies is the usual Hollywood propaganda promoting LGBTQ, feminism, New Age religion, space aliens, military recruiting, racism and climate change. It's refreshing to see a movie with an entertainment agenda. I can no longer watch the garbage produced by Hollywood. I've read that the scripts are now written by artificial intelligence (AI), which helps explain why they are so bad. There will always be a racist, queer, political activist who inputs data to the AI script writer. There will always be a Marxist, queer wizard behind the Hollywood curtain.

A lot of Thai men are fans of Muay Thai boxing. Thai boxers are respectful; they don't cheat; and they don't do all the loud mouth smack talk and public celebration when they win. Soccer is the most popular sport in Thailand. Thais seem to like the British teams the best. The Thai women's volleyball team is highly ranked, and without a doubt they are the prettiest team in women's sports. Twenty years ago, it was rare to see a fat Thai person. Coke and Pepsi have become more popular, so diabetes and obesity are now growing public health problems in Asia. Asian women tend to manage their weight as they age. There are nice looking women here at forty, fifty, and sixty years of age. Suu Kyi was still a pretty woman at age seventy. American women seem to accumulate twenty pounds with every baby they don't abort.

In Thailand there are three genders: man, woman, and ladyboy. A ladyboy is not a man or a woman. He will tell you that he is a ladyboy. They don't care about pronouns, and they don't bother anyone. At school they use the boys' toilet—elsewhere, I don't know if anyone cares. The ladyboys who can pass as women will use the ladies' toilet. I've seen ladyboys in the men's room, and no one seems to notice or care. Gender fluidity is not a fashionable idea in Thailand. Ladyboy culture has existed here for as long as anyone knows. It has always been here. In the high school where I work, I can count the number of ladyboys on one hand. They seem to be about 1 percent of the population. There are probably about the same number of lesbians. I suspect a lot of Thai men swing both ways, but they keep it discreet. The ladyboys are easy to spot because they wear makeup and hair ribbons, and have certain mannerisms. Thai schools don't allow ladyboys to wear skirts or to use the girls' restroom. Ladyboys are very popular. The boys don't bother them and the girls play make-up with them. They are outgoing, friendly, sociable, and likable. Thai fathers are disappointed with ladyboy sons, and many never accept the situation.

Ladyboys tend to work at jobs that are traditionally female. They don't work in construction, and they don't join the army. I would imagine the Royal Thai Army is under increasing pressure from the U.S. State Department to promote a tranny to the rank of general. In the shopping malls the ladyboys sell women's clothing and cosmetics, and they tend to be aggressive. Perhaps they get paid commissions. They play an important role in the entertainment districts. In the bars, they entertain male tourists, and occasionally function as bouncers. A lot of male tourists come to Thailand specifically for the ladyboys. I'll bet they don't tell their friends back home. Thailand has some of the world's prettiest ladyboys. Because they have the same parts as a man, they have an understanding about how to please a man. There is a robust medical transition industry here that offers hormone blockers, breast implants and a surprising number of body modifications. The majority of ladyboys don't cut off their money maker. There's no medical insurance for that. That surgery is expensive, and it can cause serious medical problems and lifelong pain. Besides, the penis is a big part of what the tourists want.

Of course, there are a lot of biological females working in the bars. Their job is to sell expensive drinks to the tourists. Prostitution is illegal in Thailand. What a man and woman decide to do after they leave the bar together is a private transaction. The bar fine compensates the bar owner for the loss of her employee for the rest of the day. By law the girls should be at least twenty years old, and the bar owners are supposed to check their ages. If a tourist gets caught with an underage girl, he will be deported, but the bar owner will not be questioned. The entertainment districts are safe to walk around at night, and there are few problems or arrests—it's part of the business model. Of course, some of the tourists drink too much and misbehave, but the ladyboys push them out to the street without hurting them. The entertainment districts are sort of a Disneyland for horny western men. I have met American men at the airport who fly to Bangkok every year, go straight to an entertainment zone, and stay for two weeks or until the money runs out, and they never go anywhere else in Thailand. In their minds, this is what Thailand is. These men are similar to a foreign tourist who never goes anywhere other than Las Vegas. There is a lot of bizarre behavior that goes on with the western men here. Some of them don't seem to have much experience with women in their home country. A man meets a bar girl he likes, and he might want to see this girl again. After the second round, he refers to her as his girlfriend. Her job is to get as much money as possible out of his bank account. His job is having a good time and losing touch with reality. Sometimes he wants to remain in contact with his new girlfriend after he returns to his home country. He might send her money for a family emergency. The stories get stranger from this point. On his next trip back to Thailand, he learns that the brother who his girlfriend has been living with is actually her husband. Now the western man is disappointed and angry because he feels betrayed. Some YouTube channels exist for the sole purpose of informing the world how terrible Thai women are. These men don't seem to understand the transactional nature of the relationship. They suffer from self-delusion. What is going in the mind of a seventy-year-old man who wants to marry a thirty-year-old bar girl? To find a good person, you must be a good person. For these men, bar girls are the only women available in Thailand.

A lot of the bar girls are from poor areas in the northeast provinces.

There is little economic opportunity there. A smart Thai man I know once told me that if the government would build water storage reservoirs in the northeast, the economic growth would follow. I've also read there are significant rare earth deposits in the northeast. The Thai government has always been Bangkok-centric regarding development projects. If there were good paying jobs in the northeast, a lot of these women wouldn't be working in the entertainment zones. This kind of work is high risk, and it causes lasting emotional damage. Some of the female entertainers get involved in gambling or drugs. I don't like to criticize these women. I see them as victims. Amazingly, a few of these bar girls will retire, get married, and become good wives.

The western men who stay in Thailand long term are called *expats*. Their favorite activity is complaining about Thai people non-stop, all the time. They are bored because they don't have a life. Most were losers back home, and they are losers here. They are angry because things are different here from where they were born, and Thai people don't seem motivated to rectify this situation. They are angry because they are too lazy to learn to speak Thai. They can't communicate with Thais who won't learn English. They are angry because the bar girls don't live up to their moral standards. A lot of them stay close to the entertainment districts, but sometimes they live in the real world, if they find a woman dumb enough to marry them and their pensions. I try to avoid these louts. Their goal in life is to be miserable and make everyone around them miserable. There are many good foreigners in Thailand, but you probably will not meet them in the entertainment zones. You should not trust foreigners; loan them money; or get involved with their self-created dramas.

The Thai people who live outside the tourist areas, tend to be very conservative in their thinking and living habits. The international news in Thailand is identical to the Associated Press and Reuters propaganda in the West. Biden good, Trump bad. Before that, it is was Clinton good, Bush bad. Thai people are generally in agreement with all CIA narratives and UN dictates. They don't see U.S. cable news opinionators like Joe Scarborough and Rachel Maddow who deliver endless Marxist, neoliberal tirades. The Thai media monopoly is owned by liberal billionaires. The good news is that Thai people don't automatically think all Americans are terrible people. They will generally give us a chance to prove how bad we really are. I feel so sorry for Thai women who marry some of these western idiots. Due to the liberal media reporting in Thailand, Thai people think America is the greatest country on earth, and the streets are paved with gold. I've learned to never say anything critical of the U.S. to a Thai person. They are ultra-conservative people who have a liberal political view. Propaganda always wins any argument.

Thai people tolerate liberal behavior, but they don't condone it. Most Thais don't drink alcohol. They learn about these things from Buddhism and their grandparents. Most Thai people don't have a good opinion of most Western men. They think we are fat, ugly, sloppy, poorly dressed, ill-mannered, lacking morals, drink too much, and all we think about is sex. Our reputation is well deserved, and we worked hard to earn it. The Thai people who live and work in the tourist areas, depend on the tourist economy. These Thais are extremely friendly and always smiling. They want what you have in your bank account. The western tourists think of themselves as g*ds. They have pockets full of vacation cash, and they live in advanced nations that have slave colonies and nuclear weapons. They are superior humans and they take pride in being the best. We have come to your humble little country to bless you with our divine presence and our credit cards.

Thai women who work outside of the entertainment districts are much more conservative. They are not so anxious to spread their legs for an ugly, old, fat drunk who has a pocket full of vacation cash. Most Thai women prefer Thai men, and their families most definitely would prefer a Thai son-in-law. About 5 to 10 percent of Thai women would consider a white man.

A lot of social research shows that men tend to live happier lives when they cohabitate with a woman (who is not American). This is a natural human trait. Having kids is a biological imperative for a lot of young people. It may be out of fashion, but I don't think anyone should apologize for thinking this way. For most of us, this is genetic programming. The most critical decision a man can make is whom he marries. Good men attract good women.

There are three categories of Thai women who might consider marriage to a white man: professional women who work in business or government, college students, and farm girls. I like all three, for different reasons. If she is in high school, then don't even think about it. In Thailand the legal age of maturity is twenty. If she has graduated from high school, then she is technically in fair play territory. If you meet her family, then you will be okay. For a twenty-five-year-old man, this should seem about right. These young ladies have a shared culture; they are mentally mature; and most of them would be great partners. There are temperamental and difficult women in every culture, but that's less common here. Most Asian women prefer to live a harmonious and peaceful existence. Latin women like drama. American women are vicious and mean. College girls are great because they are probably living away from prying eyes. Anonymity facilitates social introductions. When she is away at college, she is freer to talk to a white man without losing face with her family. Gossip is what a Thai woman fears more than anything. In small towns, girls are intensely watched, and she might be reluctant to talk to a white man, even if she wants to. If she is with a girlfriend at the mall, then she is more likely to talk to you. If she is at her workplace, then she might act like you are invisible. She might surprise you. She might choose the time and place, and give you the look. When no one is watching, she will show how she really thinks about you. You will see a nice smile and a friendly disposition. You have to be discreet and patient. She needs time to get to know more about you. Thai women don't make an effort to be difficult. You don't need a clever pickup line to get her attention. Just practice Thai conversation with her. Learn small talk. Hello, my name is Emmett. What is your name?

I am from America. I live in that town over there. Where do you live? Do you like ice cream? Thai people enjoy sightseeing, just like tourists. It will be a long time before she can go on an overnight trip. That's a bridge too far. No matter where you are in Thailand there are always local attractions to see. UNESCO World Heritage sites are all over the place. A Thai woman would enjoy a coffee shop that serves western pastries. There are always temples to visit. You might ask her where there is a good restaurant for Khao Soi. If you are an older man, say forty, then the female situation gets even better. There are a surprising number of beautiful Thai women in their thirties and forties who have never had a serious relationship with a man. They have never been engaged or had an abortion. Some of them might even be virgins. Some of them might be victims of their own success. Maybe she owns a business or has worked her way into a position where she is doing well financially. She takes care of her own needs and looks after her parents. All women, everywhere, are hypergamous. Genetic programming tells them they should only date across or up in the socioeconomic hierarchy. A lot of Thai women stay single because there's not enough advanced industry to support Thai men financially. Thai men who don't have good jobs are not on her radar screen. She already has many responsibilities, and she is not looking for a man to take care of.

A Thai woman looks for a man who can get along with her family and friends. He doesn't have to be wealthy, but he has to be financially secure. He needs to be friendly and polite, and show that he respects Thai people and their culture. He needs to have his act together and have a purpose in life. Thai women like a man who has goals in life. He has a purpose and a direction he follows. If he can change a flat tire on a dark road in fifteen minutes, he's a superman.

What an American woman wants is bling-bling. She wants to see the appearance of wealth. That first date better not be at Applebee's. It needs to be the most expensive restaurant in town. And she needs some lobsters and steaks in a to-go-bag for her fatherless kids at home, who are watching gangster rap videos. She has no intention of paying for any of this. If a man really wants to step up and show his manhood, he should pay the babysitter, her cousin. A used Toyota won't cut it. He needs to have an expensive import or luxury car—the newest model would be good. He needs to have a nice, spacious, and expensive apartment. He needs to be at least six feet tall, and have a minimum of nine inches in his pocket. She wants to take selfies to post on social media, showing that she is a princess. American women have extremely high and unrealistic expectations for long-term relationships. If she meets a gangster with a bag full of rocks, she'll drop her panties in two seconds.

# The King and I

In June 1946, an American film called *Anna and The King of Siam* was released in the U.S.. It is based on Margaret Landon's novel *Anna and the King of Siam* (1944), which was derived from the memoirs of Anna Leonowens, who was hired by King Mongkut in the early 1860s to be an English teacher for his many children. Landon had been a Christian missionary in Thailand. The musical's plot is about the experiences of Anna, an Anglo-Indian school teacher who claimed to be British. Anna was hired by the king, who wanted to modernize his country and get along better with the European vampires. The relationship between Anna and the King is marked by conflict throughout most of the movie. There is an insinuation that the King fell in love with Anna. Rex Harrison played King Mongkut (Rama I) and Irene Dunne played Anna. This was a very successful Broadway show and film, which was remade several times. The most recent film version starred Jodie Foster and was a sleepy waste of time. Most Americans prefer the musical version starring Yule Brenner.

What is the real story of Anna? For five years Anna and her son lived at the royal palace in Bangkok. She tutored King Mongkut's children and advised him on protocol with the West. Previously, she was married to a British military officer involved with the subjugation and looting of India. The India Rebellion occurred in 1857, her husband died, and she was left a poor widow with a young son to raise. She answered a newspaper ad for an English teacher in Thailand. As her son became older, she decided that he should be educated in the West, so she moved to Canada where she wrote her much-fictionalized memoir, *The English Governess at the Siamese Court*, published in 1870. Her publisher advised her to spice up the book and create more drama to increase sales. She desperately needed money.

Anna claimed to be the governess at the royal court, which is impossible. The subjects taught by a royal governess are Thai language, Thai law, Thai culture, military science, Buddhism and royal protocol. Anna taught the children English language, arithmetic, and maybe some western history. When she arrived in Bangkok, she could not speak Thai. By elevating herself to a higher status, she makes her character appear more important. She creates the illusion that she was an important member of the royal court, and the king depended on her advice to steer the ship of state. She creates this silly notion that Mongkut fell in love with her and behaved like an idiot, like a western man. We are supposed to believe that a king, who had a dozen wives a thousand times more beautiful and cultured, made a fool of himself in front of his court with this widowed mother. When the royal court learned of her betrayal, they were enraged. Depicting the Thai royals as ordinary buffoons is not allowed. In 1908 Thailand enacted the lese-majesty or Royal Defamation law which makes it a crime to defame or insult the Royal Thai Family.

The Thai government is very sensitive about this and closely monitors social media, and all media, to identify journalists and other Western idiots who delight in slandering the king and his family. The reason photos are not allowed at the National Museum is to prevent the social media idiots from posting photoshopped images of royal objects and images. Movie producers in Thailand are required to sign a contract giving the Thai government rights to review and edit out insults to the royal family. The Thai Royal Family are not ordinary people. They are considered by many Thais to be sacred.

One of the most revered kings in Thai history is Chulalongkorn (Rama II). He was the first-born son of King Mongkut (Rama I), and a student of Anna Leonowens. Chulalongkorn is most beloved by Thai people because he ended the practices of polygamy and slavery in Thailand. Chulalongkorn experienced the heartbreak and sadness of his mother, who truly loved the king, and she was his first wife. He also witnessed the unfair treatment of slaves who were brutalized for minor infractions or perceived disobedience. Slavery in Thailand was different from the West. Thailand did not send ships abroad to transport people in chains. Thai slaves were not de-humanized and treated like animals, as in the U.S.. They were fully human, and there were laws and customs concerning their welfare and treatment. Thailand's feudal period saw fiefdoms endlessly at war with one another for dominance and hegemony. When one fiefdom conquered another, the goal was to delete the opposing king and his family, and as many of his soldiers as necessary to achieve victory. The survivors became slaves of the new king. This process went on until the entire kingdom of Siam was consolidated under King Mongkut (Rama I) of the Chakri Dynasty. Chattel slavery had ended in Britain and the U.S., and Chulalongkorn had the wisdom to stop this practice and attempt to join the community of modern nations.

# The French Connection

From the late 1800s to 1954, Vietnam, Cambodia and Laos were part of a French colony system called French Indochina. It was operated as a slave colony in which the SE Asian people were forced to produce opium and rice whiskey for export. In the twentieth century, rubber trees from South America were introduced, which led to the Michelin Tire Company getting fabulously wealthy on the backs of these poor people. The opium was shipped to heroin refineries in Marseille, France, and then redistributed to the U.S. and Europe. The Vatican claimed ownership of all the arable land in French Indochina.

The Paknam Incident was fought during the Franco-Siamese crisis in July 1893. As a result, the King of Thailand was forced to cede to France land on the east bank of the Mekong River. He gave away Cambodia to prevent Thai people from being enslaved to these French vampires. The Thai word for France is *farang*. Today, a foreigner in Thailand who looks to be of western ancestry is called *farang*. This is not a derogatory term. It just means a person who looks to be of European ancestry. White folks all look the same. We all look like French vampires. Africans, Arabs, and people of other ethnicities are not called *farang*. They are called by their specific ethnicity. Westerners are often curious about this Thai word, and I have never read an adequate explanation for its origin. So, here it is.

During WWII, Germany invaded and occupied France, so the French vampires were temporarily forced to abandon their slave colonies in SE Asia—but the Asian drug lords continued producing opium and smuggling it to the French, and the New York junkies kept getting that good French dope. The Japanese occupied Vietnam in 1940, and were later forced out after the U.S. detonated atomic weapons over Japan in 1945. Things were starting to look hopeful for the Vietnamese slaves, but the French came back for more smack after the war ended. In 1954 the French got smacked down at Dien Bien Phu. U.S. President Eisenhower considered letting Vietnam become an independent, democratic state, which is what Ho Chi Minh wanted from the beginning. But his successor, John F. Kennedy, a Roman Catholic, promised Cardinal Spellman that the Vatican would not lose this profitable slave colony. JFK eventually got what he deserved. And the Vietnamese eventually got what they deserved, freedom from slavery and religious persecution. Let's wish the Vietnamese people well. They have suffered enough U.S. barbarism.

# Military Dictatorship?

During World War II, the Thai government signed a cooperation agreement with the Japanese, not because they wanted to, but because they were threatened with brutal occupation if they refused. Japan's primary motive for entering Thailand was the construction of a railroad to Myanmar, known today as the Death Railway. In 1957,

Hollywood made the propaganda film *Bridge Over the River Kwai*, starring William Holden, and Americans loved it. It's mostly fiction. There is a museum in Kanchanaburi where tourists can learn the truth about the atrocities committed there, and there is a Japanese WWII era train still in operation, so that tourists can ride on the Death Railway. The Erawan National Park is nearby, and there is a nice elephant camp nearby. I went to the elephant camp in 2010, and the elephant trainers were Myanmar men who all had bullet scars on their back sides, as if they had been shot while running away. In 50 years, there won't be any wild elephants in Thailand because of cross border poaching. The elephants are well treated and guarded in the tourist camps.

After the U.S. detonated atomic bombs over Japan, the Thai government quickly became a U.S. ally. During America's war against Vietnam, the U.S. gave Thailand valuable military assistance with their own domestic communist insurgency.

Thailand's political system changed from absolute monarchy to democracy in the 1932 Siamese revolution. More than ten coups occurred before the 1997 constitution of Thailand. Thailand has a bicameral parliament similar to Great Britain, with an upper Senate and a lower House. The King of Thailand does not participate in politics. He is above it. He has private meetings with the prime minister, or anyone he chooses, and if he has a strong opinion about a public matter, his wishes become law. In Thailand it is illegal to defame, insult, or threaten the King of Thailand or his family. The Royal Defamation law (lese-majesty) has been in effect since 1908.

The communist insurgency in Thailand was a guerilla war lasting from 1965 to 1983. It was fought between the Communist Party of Thailand (CPT) and the Thai government. It was the second largest communist movement in Southeast Asia, after Vietnam. The CPT was initially organized by North Vietnam.

On October 6, 1976, Thai police and right-wing paramilitary soldiers executed a crackdown against leftist protesters who had occupied Thammasat University. People on both sides were deleted—46 in all—and a student was lynched from a tree. Vestiges of the Thai communist movement are still present at Thammasat University in Bangkok, and they are always delighted to participate in violent protests against the government.

Thaksin Shinawatra, formerly a policeman, founded the telecommunications conglomerate Shin Corporation in 1987, making him one of the wealthiest people in Thailand. He founded the Thai Rak Thai Party (TRT) in 1998, and became prime minister in 2001. He was the first democratically elected prime minister of Thailand to serve a full term and was re-elected in 2005 by an overwhelming majority. His government launched programs to reduce poverty, expand infrastructure, promote small and medium-sized companies, and extend universal health coverage. Thaksin declared a "war on drugs" in which more than 2,500 people were deleted and many thousands more imprisoned.

Thaksin also took a strong arm against the Musl*m insurgency in the southern provinces, where 85 percent of residents are Musl*m. The Tak Bai Massacre occurred on October 25, 2004. The Thai military suppressed a protest in the city of Tak Bai. They rounded up one thousand protesters, stacked them face down in trucks, and hauled them to prison camps five hours away in Pattani. Seventy-eight prisoners were suffocated or crushed to 'not-alive' and several more were shot *making them* 'not-alive.' Thaksin is a tough guy.

Thaksin also tried to privatize the Kingdom's public electricity assets. Had he been successful, Thai electric bills would have tripled. He pursued any opportunity he could find to force the Thai government to apply for International Monetary Fund (IMF) loans. He was also making some moves against King Bhumibol.

In September 2006, with King Bhumibol's support, the Royal Thai Army staged a coup against the elected government of Prime Minister Thaksin Shinawatra. Facing an eight-year prison sentence for corruption and abuse of power, Thaksin left Thailand for fifteen years in a self-imposed exile. It was at this time when the Council on Foreign Relations declared Thailand to be a military dictatorship. When a nation interferes with or removes a western intelligence asset or a traitor from its government, this is an unforgiveable sin. Independent, sovereign, self-ruling nations are not tolerated by the CW. A nation can only have democracy and freedom if it is ruled by the U.S. State Department.

Abhisit Vejjajiva was prime minister from 2008 to 2011. He's well-educated, articulate, and compassionate. As of 2024, Abhisit is the last prime minister to not come from the military or be related to the Shinawatra family. Not much was accomplished, and his administration was plagued with communist protests organized by the NED. It seems his administration was criticized for not accomplishing enough to help struggling Thai people.

During his self-imposed exile, Thaksin owned Manchester United Football Club from 2007 to 2008, and lived in Britain, Cambodia, China, Dubai, and elsewhere. He continued organizing his political party renamed Pheu Thai. His daughter, Paetongtarn, is the current party leader, and she is eligible to become prime minister. Thaksin returned to Thailand in August 2023, and King Maha Vajiralongkorn commuted his sentence.

Yingluck Shinawatra, Thaksin's sister, served as Thailand's first female prime minister from 2011 until 2014. In 2011 Thailand suffered the worst flooding in modern history, which devastated the country. She presided over a number of corruption scandals, as well as a subsidy scheme that caused billions of dollars in state losses. In May 2014, the Constitutional Court unanimously removed Yingluck Shinawatra (Pheu Thai Party).

General Prayut Chan-o-cha, Commander of the Royal Thai Army, launched a coup, the twelfth since the country's first coup in 1932. The military junta calling itself the National Council for Peace and Order (NCPO) ruled Thailand from 2014 until 2019. Prayut was endorsed by King Bhumibol as NCPO leader and Prime Minister.

On January 13, 2020, Thailand was the first country outside of China to report a case of the coughing flu. Thailand was successful in containing the pandemic throughout most of 2020 using anti-viral drugs, but the virus got out of control; business and entertainment venues were closed; teachers, nurses and hospitality workers were required to take the needle; lockdown measures and curfews were implemented in varying degrees throughout the country, and the Prayut government became more unpopular. I think the Prayut administration acted in good faith. They believed the World Health Organization (WHO) is a legitimate agency, and, acting like military generals, they went along with all these authoritarian mandates. Prayut might not be aware that Tedros Ghebreyesus, Director-General of the World Health Organization, is a member of the Communist party of Ethiopia. To help control inflation, the Prayut government cut the diesel fuel tax, which provided needed relief. This shows compassion. I don't think Prayut is a foreign intel asset, unlike his political opponents. He made the best of a bad situation, and he genuinely cares about his nation. Under his leadership, Thailand was stable, peaceful, and inflation was managed.

After the lockdowns ended, and Thailand began to open back up for tourism, the Thai government considered any and all suggestions to improve the economy and put more money in the pockets of ordinary Thai people. The health minister, Anutin Chamvirakul, proposed a medical cannabis scheme wherein Thai people might grow cannabis to sell to pharmaceutical companies. Thai people would also get the many health benefits of cannabis medicines. Cannabis was legal in half the United States, so why not Thailand? In June 2022, the Prayut administration delisted both cannabis and hemp plants, their unprocessed parts, and extracts containing low tetrahydrocannabinol (THC) level (less than 0.2% by weight) and seed oils derived from cannabis or hemp plants in Thailand from the Narcotics Code, officially becoming the first country in Asia to do so. Four thousand Thai people were released from prison due to this Nixonian drug war policy. This type of compassion for people is rare in politics. For hundreds of years in Thailand, cannabis was a natural herb used in cooking and folk medicine. Anutin is currently Interior Minister. He would be my choice for PM, but he's old, and I never get what I want in politics.

If the Thai government could permit China to build the Kra Canal across the isthmus, they could generate a fabulous revenue stream, but the CIA won't allow it. The Panama Canal generates huge revenues, and Jimmy Carter gave it away. What is being proposed and studied is an overland transport corridor that will never be built, and no one wants it. The U.S. government suppresses economic development in its vassal states at every opportunity.

Protests began in 2020 with demonstrations against the government of Prime Minister Prayut. They later expanded to include demands for reform of the Thai Monarchy. The protests were organized by the Future Forward Party (FFP) which was critical of Prayut and the changes made to the Thai constitution in 2017. Their ideology was characterized as progressivism, social democracy, anti-militarism, and anti-monarchy. The leader of the FFP was Thanathorn Juangroongruangkit, former vice president of Thai Summit Group. The party was dissolved by the Constitutional Court in February 2020. Thanathorn was installed in Thai politics by the NED and the George Soros Open Society Foundation.

Thanathorn organized an armed and violent rebellion against the military and the king, which resulted in many deaths. When Thanathorn was summoned to police headquarters to inquire about his role in these violent protests, he was accompanied by ambassadors from the CW nations, who made it clear they had granted him immunity from any legal prosecution. Although he is above the law, he has been banned from any future political activity.

Pita Limjaroenrat (Move Forward Party) is Thanathorn's protégé and successor. He too was installed by the NED and the Open Society Foundation. He is currently a member of the Thai House of Representatives. He is forty-three years old, handsome, and articulate. Pita is popular among younger Thai voters, especially women, who believe he is a better alternative to the old guard of Thai politicians and generals. At the age of twenty-five, after the death of his father, Pita returned from the U.S. to Thailand to take over as managing director of Agrifood, a rice bran business run by his family. Thaksin wrote Pita's recommendation letter for Harvard. While Thaksin was still Prime Minister, Pita went with him to a UN General Assembly meeting in September 2006. Thaksin was unable to deliver his speech at the UN due to a military coup on September 19, leading to his departure for London. Thaksin probably went to London to take instructions from his MI6 handlers. Following the coup of Thaksin, upon his return to Thailand, Pita faced a brief detention. He continued his academic career by completing a Master of Public Administration (MPA) from Harvard and a Master of Business Administration (MBA) from Massachusetts Institute of Technology 2011. On May 22, 2023, Pita and his coalition partners held a press conference where they focused on key issues such as drafting a new constitution through the Thai General Assembly, implementing military reforms, introducing voluntary conscription, legalizing same-sex marriage, and de-centralizing the economy. He attended a gay pride parade in Bangkok. He thinks Thailand needs welfare programs, like the U.S. He also mentioned that his campaign strategies were inspired by Barak Obama's 2008 U.S. presidential campaign. He has cited U.S. Senator Bernie Sanders as one of his role models.

Pita doesn't actually want to de-militarize Thailand, which sounds good to a Buddhist or a utopian peace lover. He just wants to take away all political power and influence from the military, so that he can order the military to go here and go there and do this and do that, and they will have no say in anything. Pita and his U.S. handlers actually need a larger and more powerful military to fight a proxy war against China.

Despite securing a majority coalition in the lower house, Pita was unable to secure enough votes from the Assembly in the first ballot. The Pheu Thai party (Thaksin) formed a coalition with military-aligned parties in the parliament. Their unlikely alliance resulted in the youthful, pro-reform Move Forward party being pushed into the opposition, angering many voters. The communists organized more protests, but in the end, Srettha Tavisin, a close friend of Thaksin, was elected Prime Minister. Srettha likes to attend WEF meetings. Every time he returns from a WEF meeting, he informs the government about what Thailand must do to conform to WEF policies. Pita is probably right there with him in Davos to get instructions from his CIA handlers.

In 2008 Pita was named as one of *CLEO Thailand's "50 Most Eligible Bachelors."* He likes rock music bands like Cold Play, Metallica, and Radiohead. He appears to be the coolest and most likable man in politics. After the 2023 Thai general elections, Pita was named as TIME 100 NEXT by *Time Magazine*. He was the only Thai to be selected for the list in 2023. He attended the TIME 100 NEXT gala night in New York on October 24, 2023. According to results from a National Institute of Development Administration (NIDA) poll survey, published at the end of 2023, Pita remained the most popular politician in Thailand. Poll respondents stated he possesses leadership qualities, is accessible to the new generation, and has a good personality. Move Forward remains the most popular party in Thailand, with opinion souring on Pheu Thai after their collaboration with military-aligned parties in the parliament. This is what the NED does for all their candidates in targeted countries. They pay media hacks and spin doctors to write puff pieces and create opinion polls and surveys that make the candidate seem like the greatest thing since Buddha.

The Move Forward Party is today the most popular party in Thailand, and Pita has vowed that he will continue to pursue the Prime Minister position, and eventually overturn the Royal Defamation Law. The U.S. State Department, the communists, and Pita want to give the King of Thailand a treatment similar to what Donald Trump has been given by his political opponents. It begins with criticism, lies and slander. I have seen some of the gossip published about King Maha Vajiralongkorn and his father Bhumibol, and I don't believe any of it. Journalists are notorious liars and a propaganda tool of the global elites. The legacy media is a lie factory. I think Pita will be generous and sympathetic toward the king and his family, and allow them to exile to Germany or somewhere. If the king is treated too harshly, that could damage Pita's public reputation as the coolest and most likeable politician in the world. All the media corporations in Thailand are owned and controlled by liberal billionaires. They get the same 4 a.m. talking points from the Associated Press and Reuters that the U.S. media use for their propaganda. The slanders seem to be mostly about the king's lifestyle and personality. I haven't seen any information about him or his father causing harm to anyone or committing crimes. The Chakri dynasty is the royal family of Thailand, and has been in power since 1782. Maha Vajiralongkorn is the current king who ascended to the throne after his father's death. King Bhumibol Adulyadej ascended to the throne in 1950 and died in 2016. The royal family is estimated to be worth $30 billion to $60 billion U.S. dollars. Taxpayers pay for their security and upkeep of the royal residences, which are also tourist attractions, but the royal family's living expenses are paid from their personal investment assets. The globalists want to loot the royal family and put an end to their nationalist, conservative influence. When the globalist pirates decide to loot, impoverish and enslave a country, it always begins with a media campaign. When the Council on Foreign Relations says that a country is a dictatorship, or they don't share our values, or they don't obey our international rules-based order, then the U.S. State Department must take action to protect freedom and democracy, and strip the country of its assets.

Some visitors to Thailand have commented about police road blocks, particularly in areas near an international border. Thailand shares a porous border with Myanmar that is 2,416 km (1,501 miles) long. Unlike the U.S., Thailand enforces its immigration laws. People who are in the country illegally are deported immediately. These road blocks are mainly looking for illegal migrants, drug traffickers, and human smugglers. Sometimes a Myanmar man will sneak across the border, do an armed robbery, and vanish. The police could also be looking for a particular Thai man. I've driven through a hundred of these road blocks and have never been stopped, but, just in case, I always travel with my driving license and a copy of my passport, which are required by Thai law. I normally obey traffic laws, but I did get a speeding ticket once or twice. The Thai police use radar and cameras. After I got my photo taken, I arrived at a road block where I, along with five other cars, was directed to park at a highway police station to show my driving license and pay a fine. They didn't search my car, or try to provoke a confrontation, or do the extortion shakedown like U.S. cops.

Thai police are more business-like, and friendly. Another time, I got a speeding ticket in the mail, with a photo of me driving my car, and a time stamp. A Thai policeman will normally avoid contact with a white man, because he doesn't want to speak English. A white man normally has to do something really stupid and outrageous to get the attention of a Thai cop. They have better things to do. It's rare to come across a Thai cop who wants to practice speaking English. Where are you from? How long do you stay in Thailand? How many wives do you have? I was once walking on a road outside of town, and a Thai cop stopped to give me a ride. I have Thai cops as neighbors, and they've always been friendly.

Thailand is home to approximately 100,000 refugees along its border with Myanmar, and another 5,000 refugees in urban areas, almost half of whom are children. Thailand has attracted millions of economic migrants from neighboring countries. Sectors such as fishing, agriculture, hospitality, domestic work and manufacturing are heavily reliant on migrant workers for manpower. The Thai government does not have an asylum system for refugees, which is another complaint of the U.S. and UN. There is no birth-right citizenship here. The CW insists that all nations must throw open their borders and grant citizenship to anyone who crosses. The migrant children actually do have a path to citizenship. Because they grew up in Thailand, passing the citizenship test is easy for them, and there are free legal services for them. Although they don't have asylum status, the refugees have the permission of the Thai Royal Family to live there, and no one bothers them. King Bhumibol did so much for the refugees. He built the Royal Projects, which are large greenhouses and farms, so the refugees would stop growing opium, and instead grow food, trees and office plants to make money. He did this while Richard Nixon built prisons.

China is Thailand's largest trading partner among ASEAN

countries. Eleven to 14 percent of Thailand's population are considered ethnic Chinese. Thailand also does a lot of trade with Russia, and now Phuket is full of liberal Russians and Ukrainians who came here to avoid conscription.

Generally, the Royal Thai Army does not engage outside its borders. From 1965 to 1972, Thailand sent 37,644 military personnel to South Vietnam as part of the Free World Military Assistance Forces. In 2003 Thailand committed 423 non-combat troops to nation building and medical assistance in post-Saddam Iraq, and the U.S. designated Thailand as a major non-NATO ally. The Thai people were not happy about sending troops to Iraq, but Thaksin is a globalist stooge, so he had to show support for his CW sponsors. In May 2011, Thailand engaged in a border dispute with Cambodia which lasted about one month. Established in 1982, Exercise Cobra Gold is the largest joint military exercise between the U.S. and Thailand. Held annually, it has been expanded to include Singapore, Indonesia, Malaysia, Japan and South Korea. Thailand is practically a NATO member state. Thai people, being largely Buddhist, are opposed to war, but they live in a rough neighborhood, so they support a strong defense capability. Conscription is a national duty outlined in the Constitution of the Kingdom of Thailand. It mandates military service for all male citizens over twenty-one years of age who have not completed reserve training. Many Thai men avoid military service by completing reserve training in high school or college. Another way of avoiding conscription is to show up at the recruiting office wearing a dress. I've never heard of a Thai man who was conscripted against his will. Thai soldiers are all volunteers. The Thai military is used for policing its borders and to fight cross border crime, such as poaching, timber theft, and trafficking. They don't need a large military because they don't have a war profiteering industry.

# Buddhism

I was privileged to attend a monk ordination ceremony. Most Thai men join a Buddhist monastery for two weeks or longer. Some could be monks for several months or even years. When he does it, how long he stays, and the location of the monastery, are all his decisions. There are forest temples and city temples. A new monk is normally around college age, but he could be a lot younger. Sometimes he has a wife and child already. On this occasion he was an unmarried twenty-seven-year-old man whose parents had recently passed away. It is said that this brings honor to his family, especially his mother. It can be a small private affair with close family members, or in this case, it was a celebration with the extended family, friends and neighbors. There were about 200 people at this event. It was catered by the same people who do weddings and funerals. House parties are an industry here. This is a solemn religious occasion, but Thai people seem to make everything into a party. This country has three New Year celebrations. The guests typically arrive at mid-morning and are served food and drinks. Beer and water are provided, and men who prefer whiskey can bring their own. This party had a live traditional Thai band, and the musicians were talented. There was a man and a woman who both had great singing voices. They had a base player, a drummer, a man with cymbals, and there was a man who played a Thai horn instrument made with bamboo pipes. It's the same type of horn I've seen played at boxing matches. A couple of ladies were dancing, and I always join in on that. Most of the attendees were elderly family members. Several children were there as well. It was like a big family reunion. Four generations were present with a lot of aunts, uncles and cousins. My mother-in-law traveled fifty kilometers to attend. This is the town where she grew up.

The first thing that happens is what seems like a purification ceremony. All the hair is shaved from his head, including eyebrows and any facial hair. The head is the most sacred part of the human body. The guests take turns cutting his hair with scissors. This is a lighthearted and fun activity. Each guests cuts three locks of hair. Then a couple of men shave him, and he is bathed to remove the cut hair from his body. Then he adorns a ceremonial dress or covering. All vestiges of his worldly life are removed. A veteran monk arrives, and he and the initiate and close family members sit in a prayer room, and the monk recites Buddhist prayers and blessings for about an hour. Then the initiate sits in a chair in the back of a pickup with his sister, with ceremonial umbrellas, and there is a procession around the neighborhood, with the musicians leading the way in another truck, and they end at the temple. The initiate goes inside where other monks are present, and they recite more Buddhist prayers and blessings. All the guests go home, and the new monk stays at the temple, which is his new home. There is no electricity or hot water. The monks eat one meal per day and drink only water. The new monk will spend his days in prayer, meditation and Buddhist teaching. They do some chores to maintain the temple. He will lose weight. Some men might become a monk to kick a drug or alcohol addiction. Some are experiencing a life changing situation, and they need time to think without distractions. Each man has his reasons. It's usually about making his mother happy.

Westerners are mystified by this religion. Someone not born and raised here will never understand it deeply. How can you have a religion without ritual human blood sacrifice? Without ritual human blood sacrifice, the Protestant faith could not exist. Buddhism doesn't require blood-letting from any animal. Monks eat vegetarian. Killing anything is prohibited. Thai people eat fish, chickens and pigs, but most won't eat beef. A cow is considered to be an animal of higher order. It is a sentient being. Thais don't eat dogs, cats, monkeys or elephants. In China people eat anything that lives or once lived. There is very little Buddhism remaining in China. The meat-eating problem has been explained this way. Thai people eat small amounts of meat, only what is necessary for nutrition. The meat is a small portion of the dish. It is not *the* dish. A Thai would not eat a big bloody steak the way an American would. In the past a Thai could not work as a butcher. Men from Myanmar were hired for that job, the part where we take the animal's life and spill out his guts.

In a few temples, but not many, I've seen fortune telling, numerology, and astrology practiced, but this is not part of Buddhist religious practice or canon. These practices are omnipresent in Thai and Chinese folk culture. These are also common practices in American and European secret societies. These occult people hanging about at the temple are not monks. Gambling, as with prostitution, is illegal in Thailand, but the lottery is present everywhere. Some Thai oligarchs want legal casinos. Numerology is important here. Most Thai people don't practice necromancy, talking to spirits of the dead, although I have seen it in Thai and Chinese movies. I am told there are mediums who summon the dead, for a fee, but one would have to go to their house for that. There is a lot of Chinese culture here, and there are many things I don't understand.

Buddhism began in the fifth century BCE in Northeast India and spread throughout the Silk Road. It is reformed Hinduism, which dates back to before recorded history. Lord Buddha was a fully human man who was deified after death. Buddha was the earthly son of a king, and he gave up his wealth and privilege to become a monk. He was an extraordinary man who revealed important new ideas that changed society for the better. He developed a philosophy which teaches people to minimize unnecessary suffering. We bring a lot of problems into our lives with human desire, extremist thinking and immoral behavior.

Buddha taught a middle way of thinking and behaving. He overcame human desire and achieved a state of enlightenment or nirvana. He escaped the circle of re-birth and reincarnation. He escaped the worldly plane of existence, and now exists in the unseen other world with Brahma and all the other gods. It's not about man becoming a g*d. It's about escaping earthly materialism, and dwelling with the supernatural entities in the unseen world. Buddha is what every Buddhist person should aspire to become. Buddhism doesn't permit alcohol or substance abuse, which distort reality. Opium is fine as a pain reducing medicine, but not for daily consumption. Sex is necessary to make a baby, but any uncontrolled desire or extreme behavior leads to suffering. Eating is necessary, but gluttony causes illness and suffering. Buddha did not agree with the Caste System in India. This birth-right social power hierarchy is not permitted in Buddhism, but Thailand has a royal family. The Thai monarchy is an historical artifact from the feudal period. It was the required government system during that time, and loyalists would argue that the monarchy is relevant today. People who live their lives according to this philosophy are less likely to cause problems and suffering.

The royal family were dethroned and exiled from Myanmar, and that country has been at war ever since. In my opinion, the monarchy is an institution that creates stability in Buddhist societies.

Without the philosophy of correct human living, Buddhism would be about the same as Hinduism. There is a supernatural and superstitious component of this religion. The universe is run by a society in the unseen other world. There is a big G*d, Brahma. And there are smaller g*ds, like Krishna, Vishnu, Kali, etc. My favorite is Hanuman—he is the monkey g*d who can change his physical size. They seem to have a lot of conflicts in the other world. These Hindu stories are painted on murals at the Grand Palace, and tourists can read the English translations.

In Mediterranean religions, Jupiter and Zeus are the big G*ds. Aphrodite, Poseidon, Venus and Apollo are little gods. And there are g*d-man hybrids. Hercules was the son of Zeus, and he had superhuman strength.

In Christianity, there is the big G*d and a lot of angels. And there are G*d-man hybrids. Jesus is the hybrid half-man son of the big G*d. There are also hybrid human giants called Nephilim who lived before the flood. Goliath and his brothers were hybrids, but in Hebrew he was called a Refaim because he lived after the flood. There are also cherubim and other supernatural entities that serve the big G*d. And there is that bloody cross. We must have ritual human blood sacrifice.

This is a terrible oversimplification of a serious topic by someone under qualified. I want to give Americans my sense, or my two cents, about this critical factor that shapes Thai culture.

# Thai Language

Here's some good news. The Thai alphabet is almost perfectly phonetic. A written letter or letter combination always has the same sound. When I was a school boy, we learned English using phonics. The sound of the word is made by combining the sounds of the letters. This is a lot easier than learning Chinese, Japanese, or Korean.

The communist Frankfurt School gang developed a new method of teaching English called the whole language method, and they stopped U.S. schools from using phonics. I don't know if U.S. schools are still using this failed approach, but I do know that it has ruined literacy in America, especially for black kids.

Thai is much less complicated than English. England was conquered and occupied by three or four different military empires. English is a mixture of about six different languages, which results in hundreds of grammar rules to memorize. Thailand was never conquered and occupied by a foreign power. It is a single language with maybe a dozen grammar rules. Southeast Asian languages evolved from Sanskrit.

Like all Asian languages, Thai is a tonal language. The tone changes the meaning of the individual word. This is confusing for English speakers. English uses the same tones, but they are used to express function rather than meaning. To express excitement, we use the high tone. Help! Stop! Go away! When asking a yes or no question, we use the rising tone. Would you like to go for a walk? When asking an interrogative question, we use the falling tone. What time is it? The context also helps with understanding the meaning. Sometimes if we get the tone wrong, a Thai person can still understand the meaning of the word through context. More often, if we get the tone wrong, the Thai listener can't understand what we are saying. Learning the tones is challenging. It requires study and practice.

Adult learners acquire language through an analytical process. We study the structure and rules, and we practice. New vocabulary is acquired through rote memorization. We read, write and speak the word over and over, until it eventually stays in our memory. It's long hard work, and there are no shortcuts.

*Thai for Beginners* by Benjawan Poomsan Becker, emphasizes the analytical approach. This book used to be sold with a compact disc which has listening and speaking exercises. The author uses a learning approach designed for adult learners. She recommends that we start learning the Thai alphabet from the first day. Learn to read and write just like we learned the English alphabet when we were children, through repetition and practice. Like a lot of foreigners, I made the mistake of trying to learn listening and speaking, without reading and writing. All four skills need to be practiced together. It's worth the investment. By learning to read and write the Thai alphabet, you will get there faster. If you are going to be an English teacher, you need to know the Thai alphabet. Thai students learn that English letters have sound equivalents in the Thai alphabet. Thai education relies heavily on phonics.

There are excellent YouTube videos for learning Thai. I recommend finding a single channel or content creator, and staying with that same teacher. Different teachers use different transliteration systems, which confuses me. I need to see the same transliteration system all the time. There is a standard linguistic transliteration system called the International Phonetic Alphabet (IPA), but no one outside of academics uses it. Find one teaching source and stay with it. As your Thai reading and writing skills improve, you will stop using transliteration. Today, the only way I can understand the sound of a word is to see it written in Thai script.

*Immersion* means that you live in a place where the native language is the language you are trying to learn. You have more opportunity to hear and practice speaking. Immersion doesn't work like osmosis. The words don't automatically filter into your brain. There are men who have lived here for twenty years and can barely speak five words of Thai—they don't work on it at all. They are waiting for the Thai population to learn English, and they are missing out on what could be a better life. I enjoy the interactions with Thai people, and they have more respect for a foreigner who invests the time to learn their language.

# I Care Foundation

There are numerous foundations and non-governmental organizations (NGO) in Thailand. Most of them have an agenda that is not compatible with doing anything good for Thailand, but a few have good intentions.

In Thailand the primary institutions that create stability and unity are the Thai Royal Family, the Royal Thai Army, and Buddhism. The first step to cancel the royal family is to end the Royal Defamation law (lese majesty), followed by media smear campaigns and lawsuits. What these foundations do is organize conventions, often at large hotels. The organization will have an impressive globalist sounding name like World Vision, or something environmental like Save the Planet. They advertise to get young people to attend the event saying they are recruiting global young leaders to save the world and do important things. Asian parents are suckers for anything to get their kid into some program where they can advance their careers and put another bullet point on their resume. Thai people are already on board with the climate change agenda and other UNESCO initiatives. At these important sounding conferences, young people are educated about a change process that will move Thailand into a more prosperous future aligned with the advanced nations. The old-fashioned institutions, like Buddhism and the monarchy, are outdated and have outlived any useful purpose they once served.

I know a Thai man who speaks English well and seems well-read. He owns and operates an after-hours private English school for little kids. It's like a daycare with English. After a couple of beers, he will open up and answer questions about Thai culture and politics. Thai people normally only talk to close friends and family members about sensitive topics, so this was a rare opportunity for me. He told me he was concerned about changing attitudes among young people. They no longer see any value in the traditions of their parents and ancestors. Why do they need to waste time going to the temple and doing all these meaningless rituals? Why do we need religion? Why do we need a king? I knew exactly what he was talking about. I once stayed at a hotel that hosted one of these propaganda events. It was bizarre. The people operating the event had American accents, and they sounded like Scientologists with their aggressiveness and big vocabulary about leading, organizing, planning, controlling and strategizing. It was laughable, but at same time saddening to see these young people being manipulated and programmed by these NGO hacks.

I suspect a lot of foundations here are tax shelters and charity scams. They might actually do some little something here and there for some Thai kid or a poor woman in need, and then put that out on their Facebook page. It's a fantastic opportunity for virtue signaling and tax avoidance. It's usually about raising awareness and educating the masses about some important environmental cause, or human rights, or refugees, without actually doing anything. There are also a number of Western religious organizations here. No one seems to know why they are here or what they do. I have found them to be unapproachable and very private. They don't want to talk to me or save my soul for Jesus, and I look like someone who needs saving. The way missionary scams work is: They send a group of trusted church members, trusted friends of the pastor, to a country that happens to be a great vacation spot, where there is a large population of heathens who need to be saved. They organize meetings where they give out free stuff to the natives, and they take photos and videos to send back to the home church, showing the throngs of lost souls being saved for Jesus. Doing the Lord's work requires a lot of money, and Jesus needs a new jet airplane and another mansion. U.S. Christians are naïve but generous people. The financial scam (laundromat) actually takes place in America, where the money is, and the church is tax exempt. Thai people are not much harmed by it, so I guess it's all good as long as Jesus gets His cut.

A small number of foundations do good work in Thailand. Significant amounts of money actually get to people who need help. I had a personal encounter with one of these good foundations. The *I Care Foundation* was started by a Norwegian family who lived in Thailand for many years and spent a lot of time living among the Hill Tribe people, who are mostly war refugees from border states. They mostly inhabit the hilly border regions in small farming communities. The roads to these communities are unpassable without a four-wheel-drive vehicle or off-road motorcycle. Many don't have electricity. They have primary schools in the villages where they live, but the secondary schools are located in more distant, larger towns. I Care raises money from non-governmental, corporate donors in Scandinavian nations. The U.S. State Department is not one of their donors. They build dormitories at the secondary schools so the Hill Tribe students don't have to travel long distances over impassible roads. The kids live at the school. They also offer scholarship programs for students who are the hardest working, most motivated, and show the most promise. These students get a four-year scholarship to a major university. They become teachers, nurses, doctors, policemen and administrators which Thailand needs. Rural farming is hard work that offers little financial incentive. Without these farm people, us city folk would all starve to death. Children living in these communities are smart, motivated and they have good character. They deserve an opportunity for a different life. These kids go on to successful careers, and they return to these communities and do impressive things. One of the most tragic things in life is when children don't have the opportunity to realize their potential. For about a year, I was an English teacher at a secondary school with 500 students, in a poorer agricultural district, and they boarded around 50 kids from surrounding communities. During the time I was at this school, the *I Care Foundation* built a dormitory that sleeps around 20 students. It's a good building that will last a long time, and *I Care* paid for the whole thing, and furnished architectural drawings for it. *I Care* doesn't have a propaganda agenda, and they don't tell kids what to think or believe. Education is a force multiplier. Investment in a child's education yields a thousand-fold return.

# PART III
## Teaching English

# First Day at School

In Thailand, the head administrator of the school is called the director. In the U.S. we use the word *principal*. Her job concerns budgeting, administration of funds, and external affairs. She is like a chief executive officer, chief financial officer, and chief operating officer all in one. She has an assistant director who helps her with administrative duties and accounting. They are both former classroom teachers. Thai schools have a lot of reporting and paperwork requirements. Every little thing has to be documented, signed and sealed. For each subject taught, there is a senior teacher who supervises the younger teachers under her responsibility. My school normally has three to four English teachers. The administrators and teaching staff are all government employees. On Mondays they wear a government uniform. Some Thai ladies look really nice in uniform. Some of the younger teachers don't wear a uniform on Mondays because they are contractors—they are licensed teachers who are in the process of taking exams and being vetted into the Ministry of Education. They all take civil service exams to get placed in rank. As the only foreign teacher at this school, I was brought in under contract. The dates of employment on the work permit are the same as the dates on the contract. Both documents expire at the same time. The length of the contract is normally one year. The school gets a little bonus from the government for hiring a foreign teacher. The parents prefer to have their children learn English from native English speakers who have a neutral accent.

A foreign teacher will normally have 20 to 26 classroom hours per week. A normal workday is from 7:30 a.m. to 4:30 p.m., with a one-hour lunch break and another one-hour break. The normal work week is 45 hours. The administrative staff consists of two people. There is another employee who is the media administrator. He manages the school's Facebook page and serves as an information technology administrator. He takes all the official photos. He doesn't wear a uniform on Mondays, so he's a contractor sort of like me. All the teachers have other duties as assigned. Most of the other duties are about managing student activities. My supervisor forgets that I don't understand Thai, and she usually forgets to tell me about the schedule changes that occur frequently. Thai students have a lot of activities outside the classroom. At the beginning and end of each day, everyone gathers to pay respect to the flag and the church. Many decades ago, American children used to say the Pledge of Allegiance, and many schools in the South would have a morning prayer over the loud speaker. Wherever you are in Thailand, when the national anthem is played over loud speakers, you are expected to stop whatever you are doing and remain silent for the national anthem. Not doing so is a sign of disrespect. Most of the activities seem related to Buddhism. Church and school seem to happen in the same place. They have science day, Buddhist day, English day, math day, sports day, Christmas day and many others. Most Thai people don't understand the Christmas holiday with its confusing mixture of Jesus and Santa Claus. Being the only American on campus, I was asked to explain the Christmas story to the kids.

Religious holiday: The Christmas holiday celebrates the birth of Jesus Christ, the spiritual leader of Christianity. Jesus was born in Israel in the year 1 CE. More than 2 billion people celebrate Christmas on December 25th. It is also celebrated as a cultural holiday around the world.

Non-religious holiday: The character of Santa Claus originated from a 3rd century Christian monk called Saint Nicholas. Saint Nicolas became known for his kindness and generosity. It is believed that he gave away his entire inheritance to the poor and needy, and devoted his time to serving those less fortunate. He wore red clothes when bringing gifts to children.

One of the girls was chosen to translate my Christmas story into Thai and explain it to the rest of the school. I think Thai kids are confused by the co-mingling of Jesus and Santa Claus. A foreign teacher should avoid talking about religion, but the schools want the kids to learn about other cultures. I teach the English proper names of the most populous religions, but I don't go any further. If a student asks a question about Christianity, I give him the most honest answer I can. One of the boys asked me if the baby Jesus was like a Buddha baby. Good question.

Next to Buddhism, scouting is the next most frequent activity in Thai schools. The Thai government has adopted scouting nationwide as a character-building exercise. It teaches self -reliance and communion with the natural world. The teachers and students, and the director, wear their scouting uniforms on Wednesday, which is scouting day. They take the kids on nature hikes and field trips, and sometimes they pitch tents on the school grounds and stay outdoors overnight, and make a camp fire, and all that. The teachers are real scouts. They packed their cold weather gear, and went with a group overnight to a tribal village where some of our students are from. There is a nice water fall there.

The teachers seem to rotate working duty as gate greeters. If a kid does something a teacher doesn't like, he gets to be a gate greeter the next morning. Every morning there will be two or three teachers and a few students who stand at the school entrance and greet people as they arrive. It's a tradition at this school. A foreign teacher could be asked to join such activities.

When I started teaching at my new school, there was a twenty-year-old foreign exchange student there from Germany, and she sometimes worked as a gate greeter. They gave her a scouting uniform, and she participated in scouting activities. She told me she hates wearing a skirt. In fact, she seemed to have an aversion to anything feminine. She always wore a *face diaper*, and with the German accent, me and the kids had difficulty understanding her. She told me her goal in life is to become a politician. This girl was totally invested in globalist ideology. She liked satanic rock bands, but I don't think she has initiated into a cult. Every foreign exchange student I have met is from a wealthy liberal family in the CW. Foreign travel is a rite-of-passage for liberal rich kids. I never talk to anyone on international flights for fear of triggering a woke attack. The German girl left the school shortly after I arrived, and I like to flatter myself by thinking that I played a small part in her decision to leave before her contract expiration. I think she wanted to get home because the German economy was already weakening under the economic sanctions imposed by their elected green party.

The Thai teachers clean their own classrooms, doing things like sweep the floor, take out the trash, straighten the desks, clean the whiteboard. I've seen teachers sweep leaves in the yard and mop floors. The students will do these things if you have the communication skills to ask them. This school has two grounds keepers, but this a big place for two men to maintain. The school hires additional contractors for repair jobs. After I finish a class, I like to straighten the room for the next teacher. Anything electrical has to be switched off, and the windows and doors closed. Each Thai teacher has her own classroom. As a guest teacher, I move between three classrooms, so I'm always using someone else's classroom. I found that rubbing alcohol and a microfiber towel, or paper towels work well to clean a whiteboard. The dry erase ink is supposed to wipe off easily with a dry eraser or a towel, but it doesn't always work that way. The ink pens come from different factories.

All the schools in Thailand have wi-fi, except in the border areas. My school has a large wall-mounted flat-screen TV in each English classroom. With a laptop or a note pad, I can show the kids things from the Internet. I sing terribly, but the kids enjoy English pop songs. I like to start or end the class period with a song, or something entertaining. Thai people like karaoke and love songs. Their music taste has always leaned toward soft rock and popular music. A lot of older Thais still like John Denver and Karen Carpenter. I think music is a legitimate method for teaching English, but there are people who would disagree. In a TESL training class or a teacher college, we would hope that new teachers learn that different people have different learning styles, and teachers should employ different teaching methods. People remember songs from when they were children. Most of the kids enjoy this activity. Even some of the boys like music.

Karaoke can be a valuable social skill. The kids tell me which songs they want to hear. I am proud of my students for their music choices. Their taste in music is wholesome for the most part. We studied the lyrics for *"Rocket to the Moon"* by Gavin D. and *"Perfect"* by Ed

Sheeran. The music videos are on YouTube, and they have English subtitles. The students can hear and see the lyrics. I have rules for the songs I select for teaching. There can't be any profanity, nudity, drugs, sex or violence. I avoid songs with too much irrelevant vocabulary. I have a rule about love songs—it has to be a love song. Most American love songs are actually break up songs—we don't need to bring that cultural garbage here. The Thai teachers asked me to teach two or three Christmas songs. I found several Christmas songs that I wouldn't use in the classroom. I don't like *"Jingle Bells"* because it contains vocabulary that's 200 years old that nobody in the modern world uses. I don't like to waste my student's time learning about bob-tail rings and figgy pudding, and this song about horse racing. I don't like *"Rudolph the Red Nosed Reindeer"* because it has useless vocabulary about Dasher, Dancer, Prancer, Donner, Blixen, Cupid and Vixen. I like *"White Christmas"* by Irving Berlin. *"Frosty the Snowman"* would go over well with twelve-year-olds. My favorite Christmas song is *"Happy Xmas (War is Over)"* by John Lennon. I never got a chance to teach this song, but the kids seemed to like it. This song works well with a children's choir. With the Lennon song, the vocabulary is familiar, and the song has a good message, and Buddhists are generally against war. I avoid songs that are overtly religious like *"Silent Night"* or *"Joy to the World."*

I didn't come to Thailand to be an evangelist. We studied the English version of the *"Loy Krathong"* song, and most of the kids enjoyed that. There is a young musician who posts a lot of short music videos that my students enjoy, and his channel name is *The Kiffness*. He makes entertaining videos with singing cats and dogs. His videos have English subtitles, and the vocabulary is basic—these are words that we want the kids to learn. This young man is a teacher's best friend. Modern kids like media—the more the better. I teach English conversation to 500 kids in grades six through twelve. My song choice for a twelve-year-old is different from a sixteen-year-old who wants to learn love songs. These kids are willing to complete a learning exercise from the textbook, but they get tired and want to do something different. It's nice to have these music videos available, and it shows the director that we make use of the resources provided. The Thai teachers do a better job of teaching English grammar, because they can explain the concepts, and do compare and contrast using the native language. I teach English conversation, complete sentences, and karaoke love songs.

My supervisor's name is Tah. That's her nickname. Thai names are often fifteen syllables, so I just learn nicknames. I still struggle with Thai language. I learned that she has been at this school for eight years. I'm the first foreign teacher she has worked with in three years. When I joined this school, they had recently emerged from the flu lockdown. Thai schools closed for one semester and the teachers were forced to take the needle, and of course everyone in Thailand wore face diapers 24/7—everyone except me. Tah is the mother of three, and she has excellent classroom management skills. The kids do what she says. I think we have a good relationship. I have never found anything to disagree about. Her program teaches the five skills: listening, speaking, reading, writing and grammar. I met two students who can converse with me in English, so the proof of success is there. Having no experience with children, I often ask Tah for advice. I never complain about anything—I ask for her opinions. I asked if she has worked with foreigners in the past, and she mentioned a couple of men from Cameroon, a couple of guys from Germany, and an American woman who was a certified teacher. She said that foreign teachers are about half men and half women. She said foreign teachers complain a lot. She said the American woman is the only one she would want to come back. One of the German men was often angry because he couldn't control the students. That is a sign this man does not belong in teaching. In the beginning I was concerned about myself, because I tend to be moody and temperamental. I'm proud to say that I never got angry, not even once. Kids will be kids. They want to have fun, and so do I. Few men my age have the opportunity to go back to high school. Tah told me that foreign teachers like to entertain the kids and have fun. I think we clown around because we are a little nervous and lacking self-confidence.

Thai schools don't have a good opinion of most foreign teachers. The white foreigners don't take the job seriously. They come to Thailand to party, and the teaching job is just a means to extend the party. They show up late and leave early. Some don't dress professionally. Men should wear a shirt with a collar, and slacks. Tennis shoes are okay. I wear a lot of golf shirts due to the heat. It's very casual. Female teachers are expected to wear skirts. The Kenyan lady I met was wearing a nice floral print dress. She looked fantastic and she speaks Thai fluently. Her accent is mild. She gets along well with the Thai teachers. She can renew her contract as many times as she wants. School is not a day at the beach or the girlie bar. Thai teachers are professionals. Some of the foreign teachers are dodgy characters. They are lazy, and they complain about everything.

Many English speakers have poor speaking skills. Everyone has an accent, but some accents don't belong in a classroom. I have difficulty understanding Americans from the deep South and New Jersey. An English teacher must not use slang or Ebonics. I have difficulty understanding a lot of people from Britain, Ireland, and Scotland. The parents would like their kids to speak with a British accent, but not cockney. Accents are fine, but some people mumble. Arnold Schwarzenegger and Jackie Chan could work as English teachers if they wanted to.

When they talk, they open their mouths and speak clearly. I once worked with a man from India, and he talked so fast that no one could understand him. I have a neutral accent, but in the classroom I have to slow down and enunciate clearly.

In Thailand, there doesn't appear to be a frequent problem of teachers abusing children, as in the U.S. I asked my supervisor why there are job ads for female teachers only. I had forgotten there are schools in southern Thailand for M*slim girls. I asked her if she had heard stories about foreign teachers abusing students, and she said no. She also said that none of the foreign teachers she has worked with bothered the female teachers at her school. That's good to know. She didn't appreciate these questions, so I changed the subject. Most Thai schools are co-ed, with boys and girls in the same classroom. That's what the parents want. The parents also want school uniforms. I like school uniforms because the rich students and the poor students all look like students. We don't have any rich kids at my school anyway.

A foreign teacher was caught taking up-skirt photos with his cellphone. He was promptly deported. Shortly thereafter, a law was announced making it illegal to take photos of someone without their permission.

In January 2024, a sixty-four-year-old Russian man was arrested in Phuket, Thailand on the charge of child sex trafficking a minor between the ages of fifteen and eighteen. Even with the child's consent, this is a crime in Thailand, and the Thai police vigorously prosecute crimes against children, even though sometimes enforcement doesn't appear to be consistent. A few cops might prefer to solicit a bribe, cancel the MAPs visa, and quietly send him home. Most Thai people are protective of children. This country is not a friendly place for MAPs. Seventy years ago, Southeast Asia was a popular tourist destination for MAPs, but this is changing. With computers, the Internet, and databases, Thai authorities have a greater ability to identify and track MAPs. In recent years, Cambodian police have been coordinating with the U.S. Federal Bureau of Investigation (FBI) to document and build cases against MAPs and prosecute them in the U.S.—Thailand might be doing the same. MAPs should stay in their home countries in the CW, where child abuse is normalized and socially acceptable.

My school uses a textbook called *New World Student Book* by Manuel Dos Santos. This book uses Thai to teach English. It has vocabulary words and definitions shown in both English and Thai. It offers a variety of exercises that use all five skills. Each chapter has a conversation skit that the students read to me, or read with me, or listen to me read. This book has great content with a lot of artwork and photos. I have the PowerPoint files that were made for teacher presentation. The kids don't like to carry books, so they never seem to have them at school. I always have the text book on the flat-screen without using wi-fi, which is unstable at certain hours of the day. With electric power, I'm always prepared and moving forward with the text book. The Ministry of Education did well when they selected this book. As a contractor, this book saves me so much time and anguish. A new teacher doesn't have a lot of content stored away. Students can tell when a teacher is not prepared and is just making up content on the fly. With this book, I'm always well prepared and organized. But, just for fun, I sometimes like to make up stuff on the fly and do something different. "Variety is the spice of life."

One of the exercises I do is something the Thai teachers encourage. We practice meeting and greeting and small talk. These are important language skills in any culture. The boys like to practice the western handshake. They see men doing it on TV. I show them how to do it right. It has to be strong and firm. The girls don't want to be touched. Thailand is supposed to be a no-touch society. But these boys are physical, and some of them are quite strong. They like to have sports and compete. Some of the boys want me to arm wrestle with them, but that's inappropriate behavior for a teacher, so I have to decline those invitations. When I was still new at the school, some twelve-year-old boys ambushed me, and I arm wrestled six of them in row. They all cheated, but I beat them anyway. Lucky for me, none of the teachers saw this. I didn't put them down. I just let them get tired and quit. If they had six more boys, they would have beaten me. Sometimes the kids like to fight.

Sports day is a lot of fun. For two days during the cool season, the school stops all classes, and we have sports competitions. The students are divided into four teams: red, blue, green and purple. On one side of the soccer field are four sets of bleachers for the student teams. On the other side of the field are the teachers. Both sides have an all-day picnic with papaya salad and other Thai dishes. The cafeteria ladies make food for the students, and the teachers prepare their own food. About a dozen university students come to the school to help manage the sports events. The students have drums on their side, and the teachers have a sound system with music. Thai people make everything into a party. The competitions are in foot racing, volleyball, soccer, tug-of-war and sack racing. Tah is the champion sack racer at our school. During half-time they play music, the girls do silly dancing, and the boys like to do a mosh pit style of dancing. One of the boys almost knocked me down. I asked why there were no parents at this event. The parents are working, and the school doesn't have adequate security to manage spectators. In Thailand, sports are one of many activities, and not the most important priority. They don't compete against other schools or have games during evenings and weekends, like the Americans do. They don't have multi-million dollar budgets for stadiums and sports equipment. In Thailand, there's no money in school budgets for a sports laundromat.

# Classroom Management

We don't operate a fight club the way U.S. schools do. The parents expect the teachers to intervene if their kid is getting beaten up. I broke up a fight between two girls, and the mother of one of the girls wanted to know what the teacher was doing while this chaos was going on. I don't know what happened, but one of these girls was so angry that I needed to restrain her. The other girl got off the floor and ran out, and this girl started to run after her. The twelve-year-old boys watch Thai boxing on TV, and they want to play around with their friends and practice their moves. One of them hits the other a bit too hard, and it goes from there. When I first arrived at school some boys were bullying girls. I watched them pull a chair out from under a girl and spill her onto the floor. She bruised her elbow when it hit the desk top. I complained with the young teacher assigned to watch over me, and she said she didn't like it either. As a foreigner and a contractor, it's better if the Thai teachers deal with some things. I'm not very good with classroom management.

I'm trying to improve. My wife says that I'm too soft, and these Thai kids take advantage of me. My wife is never wrong. I'm not much of an authoritarian. I just have one hard rule—no boxing. The kids know I will put a stop to that in a hurry, and if a Thai teacher gets involved, they might face some kind of disciplinary action. Learning to speak more Thai is helpful, especially action verbs. Sit, *nang*. Be quiet, *niyeb*. Listen, *fang*. Repeat after me, *pood tam phom*. Don't do that, *mai dai*. Stop, *yut*.

It's important to know how to manage the school bully. Every school has one. He doesn't waste time revealing himself to the new teacher. He has a posse of boys who follow his leadership. They sit in a corner in the back of the room. Most of the kids fear him, which delights him. One day he threw powder into a fat girl's face, and I asked Tah to speak to him about it. She told me she wants to be informed about incidents. As the senior English teacher, she doesn't want to hear about something from the director or an angry parent. A Filipino teacher told me he once found himself in a dicey situation with the school bullies at a large high school in Pattaya. He was a policeman in the Philippines, so his approach to challenges is probably different from mine. The bully is popular, and he has a lot of friends. He sees the school as his territory, and he's right. I'm the newcomer, and I will soon be gone, like all the teachers before me. I avoid eye contact because I don't want to challenge him. One should never look directly in the eyes of a growling dog. I don't get confrontational or angry with him. I don't want to embarrass him or do anything negative because that wouldn't be constructive. I don't want to control him. All I want is for him to let me get through my assigned teaching exercises without disruption. He is free to look at his cell phone and play games if he wants. He can whisper with his friends. He is still playing the high school game, because this is what he is told he must do. He usually wants to get the test points, and he often uses his friends to cheat, but that's okay. I'm happy to do the reading tests with him if he wants to get the points, and I always give him a good score. I reward participation and effort. He's actually a smart kid, and he can read English. Maybe he's bored. I always greet him with a smile, and let him know that I'm happy to see him. He will change with age, and probably be in a leadership role as an adult man. He is a student like all the other kids, and he deserves my best effort. His family loves him, and I love him too. It doesn't take long for him to realize that I'm not a threat, and that I like him. We co-exist. Eventually, he will be a graduating senior; he will be replaced by a new bully, and I will be at home taking orders from my wife.

Cell phones are a challenge for many teachers, not just me. Every kid has one, and they cost a lot of money. Everyone wants the kids to have this technology. They have a dictionary, translator, camera, and a world of information right there in their hands. The problem is they also have addictive games, social media, and pornography. Taking that phone away is like taking heroin from a junkie. I tried to take a phone away from a twelve-year-old, and he put up quite a resistance, and I didn't get his phone either. Tah would have gotten that phone in two seconds. She's not soft like me. One sunny day, one of the young teachers, my handler at the time, brought in a nicely crafted wood box. It had forty numbered slots just large enough to hold a cell phone. She placed the box behind the desk and told the students to put their phones in the box. This was a message from the director. She made those kids understand that if they continued with the games and social media, this is how it's going to be from now on. We only take the phones when we see improper usage. As a teacher, it's difficult to compete for a student's attention when he's got all that entertainment in his hand.

## Teaching Strategies

Being a teacher is challenging. It challenges one's leadership and teaching skills. If things aren't going well in the classroom, maybe the teacher has something to do with it. Maybe we should be accountable to ourselves, and be honest. Am I missing something? Could I do something better or differently? The school where I work is located in an agricultural community. I think one or two future doctors and engineers will graduate from this school. I am certain there will be a lot of nurses, teachers and business people. Once they leave school, a lot of these kids will never speak English for the rest of their lives. They know it, and I know it, but we have to get through this together. The

Ministry of Education requires every student to learn English every year. I think English should be an elective in grades 9 through 12, but I don't make the rules. The boys especially don't have any interest in learning English. I think they would be more interested in a driver education class, home economics, occupational safety and health, carpentry or something more useful for their lives. It's difficult to motivate them, and it's difficult to compete against the cell phone. It's not easy to be entertaining and capture their attention. We have the best text book, but it can't compete with that Internet gadget. Each grade (*matayom*) six through twelve has sub-grades: one, two and three. The more motivated students are in sub-grades one and two, and we have a lot of good classes with these students. They participate and try to have fun with it. Sub-grade three has the more challenging kids. It's not about intelligence. It's more about motivation. Some of these kids don't have any plans or goals. I think a lot of the boys will go into agriculture or construction, and a lot of the girls will be homemakers. There's nothing wrong with any of that. Society needs all these people. There are always a few kids in sub-grade three who don't belong there, meaning they actually want to learn English. I could be happy playing music videos and singing songs for forty minutes, but if there is just one kid who wants to learn, then I will go through the text book and teach that class for that one kid while the others surf the Net.

Content needs to be socially relevant. We need to talk about situations that the student is already familiar with or has a need to learn about: shopping, cooking, doctor's office, traveling, meeting new people, using technology. The textbook *New World* does all that.

With Tah's approval, I have used Thai literature to stimulate interest. I find a book, movie, or cartoon that has both Thai and English, and we read it, watch it, and talk about it. I have the book *The Story of Tongdaeng* written by King Bhumibol. It is a biography of a pet dog.

It's very interesting and well written, and it has lots of great photos of cute puppies. The story is printed in both Thai and English. I ask the students to read the Thai story. And then we read the English translation together. When they see the story in English, it should be a little bit familiar to them, because they just read the story in Thai. It's teaching about something the mind already understands and can relate to. There is relevance and connectivity. The students seemed to enjoy *The Story of Tongdaeng*.

They enjoyed the movie *Suriothai* which was produced by a member of the royal family. It's a historical narrative about a critical era in Thailand's feudal period. The kids already know the history, but it's possible they have never seen this movie. I have the original movie with English subtitles. I think this was a successful trial using literacy and media. If I should ever do private tutoring, I will try this *literacy approach*. Netflix has a lot of movies that offer Thai subtitles. If possible, I would use literature or movies that are specific to the student's interests and preferences. There is a man who taught himself to speak Spanish by watching 500 times a Marvel comics movie with Spanish subtitles. If I work with a young man who enjoys motorcycle repair, then I would try to find a motorcycle Owner's Manual printed in English and Thai.

I sometimes employ a teaching tactic I call strategy of tension. I use social tension to get the student's attention. While we are learning new vocabulary, I ask the students to pronounce the Thai words for my learning benefit. I read the Thai word back to them, and if I don't say it exactly right, they correct me. It's a role reversal that the kids enjoy. They get to be the teacher, and I am their student. It disrupts the normal classroom expectation. The kids are entertained by watching me struggle with learning Thai while I make funny faces. I get their attention.

I might ask them questions of a personal nature—questions they don't expect from a teacher. I once asked a girl if she wants to get married. She emphatically stated that she has no desire to get married. I asked her if she would like to have a baby. "No way!" was her answer. I told her that she is an intelligent young woman. Every eye in that classroom was on me at this point. Even the boys playing computer games looked up to watch the unfolding situation comedy. Normally, when I play act the meeting and greeting exercise, I move into small talk. I might walk over to one of the girls and say "Hello, my name is Emmett. What is your name? You're very pretty." Thai girls like to be told they are pretty. "I saw you from over there, and I wanted to come and talk to you because you are so pretty." At this point, the conversation is getting a little inappropriate. An old man shouldn't be talking to a school girl this way. The boys looked up from their video games, and every eye was on me. We have social tension. Now that I have everyone's attention, I can ask them if they have brothers and sisters. Do you have a dog or a cat? I have one dog and two cats. My dog's name is Junior. I often write these sentences on the white board as a learning reinforcement. The Thai teachers want me to engage in conversation and teach complete sentences.

# Conclusions

It's possible to make a career as a foreign English teacher. Global demand for English teachers will continue throughout our lifetimes. It's possible to obtain a Bachelor of Education through an online degree program. Becoming a certified teacher is the path to better pay and working conditions at international schools. At private schools, it's possible to apply oneself and get promoted into management positions.

This can be challenging and difficult work. Not all of us are cut out for this. It depends on the individual.

My life before Thailand was spent working in organizations with large numbers of people. My life had a purpose, maximizing shareholder value. I was a wage slave, and I was socially dependent on that lifestyle. One can never really have friends in a corporate environment, but I interacted with a lot of people, and I had a busy mind. I was never happy working in an authoritarian hierarchy with a gang of sociopaths running things. After I retired and moved to Thailand in 2018, I spent my days doing yard work, and working off an endless honey-do list. I don't enjoy endless travel and vacation like a lot of foreigners—I just want one or two short vacations a year. I've met people here who travel constantly, and I think that's great, but it's not for me.

Teaching has benefited me in several ways. Working with 500 high school students is a deep dive into Thai culture. I'm again working in an organization with a large number of people. My mind is busy. I am presented with many new challenges to overcome. Thai people are less of a mystery to me now. I feel closer to their culture, and I have a better understanding of how they interact and perceive the world. Playing with other people's children is a lot of fun. I'm not sure I would enjoy working at an international school. I feel fortunate to work with the kids in my community. These kids have helped me improve my language skills, and they have taught me things about life.

I would encourage prospective foreign teachers to search for videos on YouTube, and hear what practicing teachers from all over the world have said about their quality of life. In the beginning, it's difficult to adjust to a new culture. We have all experienced culture shock. There comes a time when the foreigner feels overwhelmed and mentally and physically exhausted by so much change in such a short time. The assimilation process begins with the honeymoon period. Then we go into the crisis period. Then comes the recovery period. Finally, we move into the adaptation and adjustment period. With the passage of time, the shock fades and our adopted country becomes our new home. If you are feeling a little depressed, then do something to get your mind off your sadness, and try to avoid too much alcohol. Cook some foreign food, go on a trip, watch some Netflix movies. If you don't like Thailand, then go to Vietnam, Russia, or Albania. I can't return to the U.S. because I experience reverse culture shock when I go back to that lawless dystopia. American society has become mean, hostile and corrupt. The oligarchs have succeeded with their social transformation of the U.S.. There's too much insanity and drug addiction. Food is over-priced and of poor quality. Housing is over-priced. Everything is over-priced. The U.S. is a poor value for me. The stress of trying to survive rising inflation and constantly being a crime victim is too much to bear. The authoritarians have become too overbearing. I can't stand what the U.S. has become. I'll just stay here and play with Thai kids, look at beautiful women, and grow tomatoes.

# Message to Christians

If this were Germany in 1930, and you were a J*w, I would beg you to leave the country as soon as possible. The Holocaust actually began as a deportation program. The N*ZIs encouraged the J*ws to go to Canaan. They were allowed to take their financial assets and any other belongings with them. Some did leave. The first European J*wish migrants arrived in Canaan on N*ZI ships. We know what happened to the ones who refused to leave the comfort of Europe.

The U.S. government has made it abundantly clear they are anti-Christ. This Christ hating sentiment is growing daily. Maybe you believe you will be raptured. Maybe you think G*d is going to protect you and your family. J*ws and M*slims believe that Christianity is idolatry. They say, "There is one G*d, and there can be no other." You are not going anywhere because right now you are comfortable where you are. You have G*d on your side, G*d's chosen people always win, and you don't want to miss the next Super Bowl.

It might be to your benefit to learn about the seven Noahide laws. These were the laws given to Noah after the flood; therefore, they apply to every human born since then, and they are recognized by the U.S. Congress and the UN as the law of the land. One of these laws is a prohibition against idol worship, and Christianity is considered to be idol worship. The non-J*ws who choose to follow the Seven Laws of Noah are regarded by J*ws as Righteous Gentiles who are assured a place in the World to Come. If a government authority asks you what your religion is, you should tell him you are a Noahide. If a government goon asks if you are a Christian, without hesitation say *no*. Cross your fingers behind your back and deny Christ a thousand times, if necessary. Sign whatever papers they put in front of you. If they arrest you, then you will lose your agency, and you will lose your ability to help yourself, your family, or anyone. That day is coming. The Torah has plenty of patriarchs telling lies to their enemies. In Genesis 20, Abraham told King Abimelech that Sarah was his sister. Lying to a government authority is never a sin against G*d, nor is it a violation of the Seven Noahide Laws. If your preacher has never talked about these things, he is probably a Freeloader, as are most preachers. One of the Ten Commandments says thou shall not bear false witness. That means giving false testimony against someone in a court of law, or signing an affidavit to get someone to be unfairly persecuted. What those Hollywood prostitutes did to Harvey Weinstein is a sin. What that nasty woman in New York City did to Donald Trump is a sin. Lying to a government goon who wants to harm you and your family is not a sin.

You don't have to be a Zionist to win G*d's favor. If you think dropping bombs on unarmed civilians is a good idea, then you might be worshipping the wrong god. I would caution people about hating M*slims. Most of our ideas about M*slims come from media propaganda and Freeloader preachers. G*d told Abraham that many nations would descend from his first son Ishmael. It seems like G*d has a plan for these people. They certainly got all the artesian oil wells. I've worked with some M*slims, and they were decent people. I would never do anything to harm them. Before the Nabateans (largest Arabian tribe) became Islamic, they were Christians who lived at Petra in modern Jordan. The Romans had become so abusive that the Arabs divorced themselves from the Roman religion, and made their own nationalist religion centered at Mecca, in modern Saudi Arabia. The Quran is a plagiarism of the Bible, and no one hides this fact. The Quran is the seventh century Bible with a little editing and some Arabic language sprinkled in. M*slims believe that Christ was a prophet, and he was fully human. Most J*ws don't even accept the idea of Christ as a historical person, because that history was written by Romans. "There is one G*d, and there can be no other."

Maybe you read this book with a young person in mind. I would rather have my child teaching English in a foreign country than lying dead on a battlefield in Europe or the Middle East. Military conscription will return to the U.S. The U.S. military keeps falling short of their recruitment needs, and the appetite for war is getting stronger. I don't think most of the migrants will join the military, and I wouldn't want to be on a battlefield with them. A lot of young American men are refusing military service. The military recruiting propaganda isn't as effective as it once was. Young people are figuring things out, and they don't want to die for greedy oligarchs and soulless politicians. Some of them don't want a queer for a commanding officer. Many young Americans don't share the same values as the Pentagon generals, who wear dresses and look at child porn on their computers at work.

www.ingramcontent.com/pod-product-compliance
Lightning Source LLC
Chambersburg PA
CBHW070248290326
41930CB00042B/2859